I0840751

Globalist Traitors,

Dig Your Graves!

by

Eric F. Magnuson

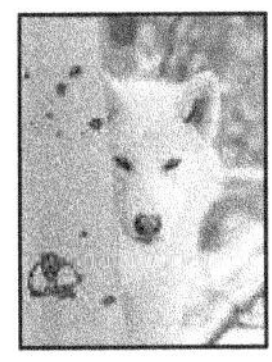

Fimbul Winter Books

Globalist Traitors,

Dig Your Graves!

ISBN: 9781792056031

Globalist Traitors,

Dig Your Graves!

When the main threats to individual
liberty center around the impending loss
of national sovereignty and the
destruction of indigenous races and
culture, them nationalism, by any means
necessary, including war, becomes the
first principle.

Sentinels of Winter

In different areas of endeavor we serve
Libertarian Nationalism, indigenous
populations, total resistance to globalization,
central bank nationalization, and unflinching
population control. We hope to teach about the
prosperity and peace that follow from natural
order, but are part of a revolution that will
prevail by any means necessary. Humanity will
not be destroyed by subhumanity. Servants of
oppression, dig your graves! Winter is coming.

Table of Contents

...SIC MUSIC. SEND YOUR KIDS TO SCHOOL.
FOLLOW FASHION, ACT NORMAL.
WALK ON THE PAVEMENT, WATCH T.V.
SAVE FOR YOUR OLD AGE.
OBEY THE LAW.
REPEAT AFTER ME: I AM FREE.

To All the Heroes of the
Libertarian Nationalist Revolution

Alternative to IMF Banks

One thing can give us worldwide liberty, prosperity, and peace, quickly eliminating the imagined need for Globalism, Socialism, and Communism. That is to get counties everywhere to pull out of the IMF, and nationalize their central banks. General education is the first step. Once the truth is well known, implementation will follow. The material below explains the entire business with succinctness and clarity:

Most of the big problems on Earth are caused by International Monetary Fund (IMF) bankers who, via privately owned member central banks, like the US Federal Reserve, manipulate currencies, and with the help of subverted politicians, engineer wars and economic upheaval so they can lend money to governments for military mobilization and otherwise unnecessary social programs. Globalism, the New World Order, is simply the one world government that will allow the IMF banks to have total finance monopoly.

Countries do not need to borrow from IMF banks, but can have their own central bank, and control their own currency. Populations are kept from the knowledge of this by cooperating mainstream media, and by subverted politicians who keep IMF control in place by voting for it in legislatures. All that is necessary to have enduring liberty, prosperity, and peace on Earth is to get counties to leave the IMF, set up their own central banks, and tie the amount and value of currency to receipted hours of work, or a mixed store of scarce and durable commodity, the value of which is determined in free world markets.

In the U.S. these changes will eliminate the unnecessary federal income tax, which pays only the interest on the unnecessary national debt. All fiscal expenditures are paid for by excise taxes at state, county, and municipal levels. See the U.S. national debt at the link below.

War and terrorism are a complex study, but the purpose of most war today is to generate 'refugees' aided by the EU and UN to invade countries to destroy indigenous race and culture, so that people lacking identity will except globalization. Terrorism is supported by deep state funding, open borders, and police stand-downs, to make daily life seem so dangerous that we will gladly surrender guns and liberty just to feel safe. Good people need to become proactive about building a better future. We will be rid of these problems only when the Globalists and their invading hordes are just a dreary memory.

* * *

We have just received two comments from France:

"It *is* succinct. All we need with this, are the addresses of those who readers must petition to produce these wonderful changes. It's really a wonder that such massive public fraud could have on for so long in plain view." ~ Brett Manteaux

"We must urge people not to vote for any politician who will not take a direct stand against further involvement with the IMF." ~ Emile Bonvuar

Introduction

This volume contains our more recent essays on the threat of globalization. Globalist bankers, media bosses, and politicians are equivalent in their effect upon society to rats carrying bubonic plague. Widespread knowledge of this, fused with the principle of leaderless resistance, will, with imagination and diligence, spell their inevitable demise.

War and terrorism are a difficult study. Just when you think you understand an event, new information surfaces showing that it was actually a false flag, usually involving Globalist traitors in your own government working with foreign operatives.

Besides Globalist banker lending, facilitated by cooperating politicians and media, the ongoing wars in the East are waged to generate "refugees" to invade and destroy indigenous race and culture everywhere, so that people lacking identity will accept globalization, and with it, corporate monopoly. The purpose of small scale terrorism is to make the everyday environment so perilous that we will gladly surrender liberty just to feel safe. We will be rid of every major problem in modern life when the Globalists, and if their invading outlanders, no longer exist.

Contents:

The short sections on evolution are included to resolve the unwarranted conflict between science and religion. We have bigger fish to fry. What this means will be clear after reading the material.

In "State of the World 2034" the reader experiences how it will feel to be living after the essential changes have been made. It's the "Ten Steps" reformatted to be after the fact.

Eric F. Magnuson

Update
November 11, 2022
12:14 P.M.

What Evolution Is

Evolution is the process by which living organisms adapt to their environment through change. This is necessary for survival, because the environment itself is always changing. If this happens so quickly that creatures can't keep up, they perish. Rapid environmental change usually has to do with temperature or water levels.

Genes are the cellular component within living organisms responsible for the characteristics of the organism. Genes themselves are continually changing. This process is called mutation and occurs randomly, but is sometimes triggered by environmental stimuli (e.g. increased solar activity).

When a creature's mutating genes result in a characteristic which favors adaptation to the environment, then the creature will live longer and reproduce more. The favorable genes are passed along to the offspring. If the opposite occurs, and the genes are not favorable to survival, then the creatures will die younger and reproduce fewer offspring, so the unfavorable genes are not passed on. This process is called natural selection, or survival of the fittest.

Science isn't science without proof. There are six proofs for evolution:

1. Universal Genetic Code

2. Continuity of Fossil Record

3. Interspecies Genetic Commonalities

4. Prenatal Growth Recaps Phylogeny

5. Postnatal Imprinting Recaps Phylogeny

6. Bacterial Resistance to Antibiotics

Note:

For detail on five of these proofs see Richard Peacock's site "Evolution: Frequently Asked Questions"

What Evolution is Not

Ever since Charles Darwin first explained the evolutionary process, there has been an unnecessary unwarranted feud raging between the religious and scientific communities. There is no real bone of contention here, and never has been, for three reasons:

1. Evolution is not a theory to be debated, but a proven scientific fact.

2. The fact that most observable phenomena are not mentioned in ancient scriptures, does not render them nonexistent.

3. Evolution does not negate the process off intelligent design. It is simply the means by which intelligent design is implemented. Universal intelligence is simply the potential for manifest existence residing in unmanifest existence (e.g. the light bulb before Edison). Natural selection unlocks this potential in the same manner as does an inventor. Both universal intelligence and technology are infinite, so there is a great deal to look forward to. See more about this ahead.

For the Libertarian connection to evolution, here are two root definitions from "Evolutionary Psychology."

1. Evolutionary destiny is the imperative for the unimpeded, ever more varied and complex expression of universal intelligence through evolving organisms.

2. Liberty is the inalienable birthright of every living organism in the universe to manifest justly as a participant in evolutionary destiny. This manifestation, to be both Libertarian and just, must not unnecessarily interfere with the evolutionary expression of any other living organism.

Seek and Destroy!

When the main threats to individual liberty
center around the impending loss of national
sovereignty and the destruction of indigenous
races and culture, then nationalism, by any
means necessary, including war, becomes the
first principle.

Sleepwalkers of the World, wake up! Forget your limp-wristed religious fantasies, alcohol intoxication, drug dreams, idiot ballgames, and virtual-reality heroism. Stand up on your feet like real men and women, think about the future, and show some proper adult seriousness for once in your pathetic lives. The eleventh hour is past. World Libertarianism is the only viable alternative to globalist oppression. All the nonsense you think matters is of no importance, and never has been. If you feel insulted by all this, then you are one who needs to read further. If not, you are probably smiling at this moment, as we are.

Fully educated people know that a multiplicity of free sovereign nations competing in a free world market has a natural workability superior to any form of world government, and can be less easily subverted to collectivism. World problems will not be solved through ignorance. Join us grownups in the Twenty First Century. Read further, so that when the smoke clears you will be worthy to smile along with us, as one who has participated in the throwing down of Globalist tyranny. Embark upon the Greatest of All Quests: Liberty Triumphant and Eternal!

Freethinker

Knowledge and Belief

Preliminary Principles:

1. An actuality is a pure state of existence apart from the perception of it by any living organism.

2. A reality is the accurate perception of an actuality by any healthy living organism. This will be qualified to some extent by previous experience and by the perceptual apparatus of the organism.

3. A fact is the conceptual representative of a reality.

4. Facts are the building blocks of correct thinking.

5. Logic is the process of correct thinking, the natural method used to arrange the building blocks provided by facts.

6. Knowledge is the correct natural correlation of facts by means of logic, the finished structure.

7. Truth is the broad and meaningful apprehension of knowledge.

8. Wisdom is the loving and just reaction to truth.

9. A belief, in the pure sense, is an attempt to extrapolate beyond what is known.

10. The amount and strength of an individual's beliefs is inversely proportional to the amount of his knowledge.

11. Philosophy is used to create a feeling of personal integrity and wholeness by attempting to extrapolate beyond available facts. Correct reactions are based upon facts, not upon philosophy.

12. Most philosophy is merely the "explanation" that people lacking facts offer to justify their own particular emotional reaction to their environment. The only worthwhile philosophy is a comprehensive overview of all available factual data fused by love, heroic idealism, good moral character, and courage. This involves an eclectic approach to the attainment of wisdom, not a slavish adherence to "isms" of any kind, including the fashionable zeitgeist of well entrenched science.

Viable Spirituality

In this context, spirituality is differentiated from religion, because it represents something much larger. It includes all of a person's values as these are reflected by actual conduct over the course of a lifetime, rather than by the mere parroting of religious doctrine, often with partial adherence. A person's spirituality comprises everything in life. This may include religious activity or no religion at all.

A truly viable spirituality must have perfect integrity between three basic components:

~ an intellectual premise consistent with all known science
and which grows along with science

~ a moral premise reflecting absolute Libertarian reciprocity.
This means no unjust encroachment against any creature or
the environment to the detriment of any living thing. This also
means absolutely no tolerance of such encroachment from
others.

~ a source, not of dogmatic belief, but of archetypal
inspiration, grounded in one's own ancestral mythology.

Absolute separation of church and state is impossible
because what the people are spiritually determines the type
of government they will create or condone. Wherever we find
the institutionalized lassitude of cowardly religion, we also
find Socialism or some other unworkable form of collectivist
government. We can't expect an inferior prevailing spirituality
to result in a superior way of running society.

Evolutionary Spirituality

This is spirituality based upon evolutionary principles. It will
evolve as society grows in understanding. It will transform
the world by inspiring people, first to cast off the chains
which bind them individually, then to democratically throw
down unjust governments everywhere. This is inevitable, but
will happen only very slowly through ongoing education
about what works and what does not.

Those who claim that human salvation can only be attained
through obeisance to some popular savior or another are
lying, although they usually believe they are not. The
confusion and divisiveness these spiritual monopolists
create with their bigoted power-hungry scheming is the one
of the most destructive forces on Earth.

Salvation comes though living in accordance with truth and
though the practice of righteous Libertarian principles.
Simple human decency is what will save the world, not
mindless belief in tepid, limp-wristed mythologies.

Popular religions more or less advocate a morality based upon non encroachment against others. This is a good start, but he reason these religions have not saved the world is because they mix this moral truth with mythological falsehood and insist upon absolute literal belief. People see through much of the falsehood and then wrongly reject much of the moral truth along with the falsehood.

Personal Obstacles to World Liberty

There are many falsehoods that seem to give fulfillment in the short term, but which deliver absolutely nothing in the long term. They are only fantasy, and a complete waste of time. Dealing with reality is far more exciting, and produces constructive change, because attention isn't diverted away from things that really matter. The main problem areas are:

1. False Beliefs
One need not embrace ancient fairy tales as literal truth in order to live a moral life. This is not to say that good principles cannot be illustrated with traditional stories and allegories. We simply need to sort out what is real.

2. Non-Libertarian Economics and Politics
Collectivist systems simply do not work. All fully educated people know this. False systems include Communism, Socialism, Democratic Socialism, Social Democracy, Democracy not constituted upon Libertarian principles, Fascism, Populism, Theocracy, etc.

3. Controlled Media
Most easy-to-get information is controlled by those in service to globalist bankers and their subverted government lackeys, re-elected decade after decade by an ignorant apathetic majority. One must seek further for hard knowledge upon which to make important decisions.

4. Drug Induced Euphoria
If you don't like environmental circumstances, change them with action, not merely your experience of them by ingesting

chemicals. Alcohol is used to suppress the cerebral cortex in order to liberate the reptilian complex. It gives timid people false courage in business and romance. One need only affect a reconciliation between Jekyll and Hyde in this regard. Psychedelic drugs seem interesting because they give the user a strange mental life. Since all human societies are based almost entirely upon lies, reading books and learning truth will give a far stranger mental life without bad side effects.

5. Spectator Sports
Ball games are just arbitrary simian competitiveness, a wishy-washy substitute for those afraid to get involved in things that actually matter.

6. Virtual Reality
Millions today resemble those poor souls who freebase cocaine, sitting all day addicted to their own brain chemicals, playing video games which give false feelings of heroism in seeming to defat enemies that do not exist. Wake up! There are real enemies to defat.

7. Excess Entertainment
Novels, movies, and music are great, especially when they inspire heroic Libertarian ideals and action. The amount need only be in balance with the other demands of real life.

8. Unproductive Friendships
This involves not wasting time with fools who suffer from any of the above delusions. Friendship should be casual and light hearted, centered around the mutual love of causes, professions, or hobbies. Meddlesome busy-bodies who encourage validation of life strategies through consensus should be avoided. It is always best to keep one's own council in order to develop inner resources. If you need advice, seek what the greatest minds in history have said, not some doped-up joker you knew in high school. Remember what George Washington said,
"Have no intimacy with worthless men."

Libertarian Basics

The Basic Libertarian Premise: It is wrong to unjustly encroach upon any creature or the environment to the detriment of any living thing. Most people agree with this premise. The disagreement is over what constitutes encroachment.

The innate love of liberty and the concession of this to others is what we may call the Basic Libertarian Impulse. Depending upon the degree of spiritual development, the individual either manifests this or does not. We know that it is unjust to unnecessarily kill, assault, coerce, rob, defraud, slander, or otherwise encroach upon any living creature. Calling these acts by other names and programming an ignorant majority to agree that they are necessary or permissible does not change their nature. To do evil is to trespass unnecessarily upon the liberty of any living organism. Historically this principle has been called the Golden Rule.

In human affairs we accept the premise that is desirable for people to reach their natural level of prosperity and development through their own volition while living in peace and harmony with each other. A human being is an creature which comes into this world with no rights owed him and no obligation incumbent upon him, except the natural right to absolute individual liberty, and since he is not alone on the planet, the logical obligation of reciprocity in this towards others. He need only concede to others the same liberty that he demands for himself, because this is absolutely all that is necessary for continuing harmony on Earth. The one human responsibility then is simply to never make unjust encroachment. The only legitimate function of government is to enforce this natural obligation of humanity. Any person or government attempting to impose any burden other than this upon the individual is guilty of criminal coercion and should be regarded as a mortal enemy even if the oppression is sanctioned democratically.

Liberty is the natural right of every living organism to manifest justly as an unimpeded participant in evolutionary destiny. This manifestation, to be just, must not unnecessarily interfere with the evolutionary expression of any other living organism.

Every problem in every society on Earth can be traced back to a point where someone in government decides to sacrifice individual liberty for some other goal. Like any breech of natural law this produces a distortion. One compromise seems to justify another and soon the cause and effect relationships become obscured by time and complexity. The achievement of harmony on Earth simply involves eliminating the complex of false dependencies that have arisen because of these past mistakes.

Individual liberty is the innate right to be free of unjust encroachment from others. It doesn't matter if the others outnumber us, are organized, and use euphemistic terminology. There are two types of unjust encroachment against individual liberty, illegal and legal. From a Libertarian standpoint both are equally as criminal. Un-Libertarian elements will allege that legal crimes are not unjust because they are determined to be necessary by a majority opinion and that this should supersede any objective measure of workability and rightness. There is no reason for decent people to compromise about this. People who don't want to be free are cowards. People who keep others from being free are criminals. The majority of people on Earth have always been and still are both.

People who have little regard for individual liberty will think that anyone who questions their morality or basic understanding in this regard is being terribly unreasonable. For those, however, who have a heroic vision for future societies, liberty is not a question to be begged, but a moral absolute. It is not negotiable or compromisable. Its value is not merely theoretical or just a "matter of opinion". The Libertarian position is the only viewpoint which is not unreasonable. The people who now oppose individual liberty eventually will be vanquished. Natural order will prevail. The first line of attack is education.

Libertarianism is not power hungry politics, but the structuring of human affairs in accordance with natural law. Anarcho-Capitalism is not chaos, but the one and only system of economics which implements natural order.

The individual has the natural right to live in a free society, failing this, to live in liberty within any society in which he may find himself, regardless of the "consequences" to anyone else. Absolute individual liberty is the one and only thing worth fighting for. The truly Libertarian position is superior to all others, intellectually and morally. There are few however, who really understand or practice Libertarian ideals. No existing government and very few people will knowingly allow complete liberty to anyone if it seems to suit their purpose to do otherwise. If the individual wants liberty, he has to reach out and take it at any cost, must guard it jealously, and to keep it must be willing to fight even unto death.

No matter what else man accomplishes, if he does not immediately deal with the problem of increasing population, nothing else he does will matter. Couples who have more than two children make direct encroachment against all other creatures on this planet. The ideal population level on Earth was passed hundreds of years ago, if by the word "ideal" we mean a level consistent with concepts like individual self-actualization and opulent joy in living, rather than mere subsistence in anguished mediocrity. Evolutionary destiny is served through qualitation, not quantification. Maximum joyful manifestation for small numbers is superior to minimum meager manifestation for vast suffering multitudes. We are not imbued with life merely to endure it.

Trying to make the world Libertarian through writing is like holding a message in a bottle while standing upon a high precipice overlooking the vast expanse of limitless ocean. You are at the brink of heroic destiny, but casting your message into the sea of fate. The message is a knowledge of natural principles, which if generally acted upon by mankind, will ensure worldwide prosperity and peace, the unimpeded evolutionary expression of all living things. You wonder if the message will ever be read by anyone. Your only certainty is that little perceptible change will result in your own lifetime, because there are few who would comprehend the message even if everyone did read it. You wonder if the message will be preserved long enough to make any difference at all or whether the life you have spent has simply been wasted. Then you wonder if anything matters at all. Then you contemplate the other things that you might have done with your life and you realize that there is nothing, nor could there ever be anything, more excellent than this: the Greatest of All Quests.

Essential Facts for World Liberty

"Let me issue and control a nation's money and I care not who writes the laws." ~ Mayer Amsche Rothschild ~

"If the American people ever allow private banks to control the issue of their currency, first by inflation, then by deflation, the banks…will deprive the people of all property until their children wake up homeless on the continent their fathers conquered…. The issuing power should be taken from the banks and restored to the people, to whom it properly belongs." ~ Thomas Jefferson ~

"We are on the verge of a global transformation. All we need is the right major crisis and the nations will accept the New World Order." ~ David Rockefeller ~

Weed Out Falsehood

We are tired of crackpots who claim that predatory globalist bankers are aliens from outer space or another dimension. It seems more likely that those who say these things are working to engineer popular mistrust of the resistance. Additionally, since it is primarily events of the past two centuries which affect us now, the endless attempts to trace all this back to ancient Egypt or reconcile it with ancient prophesies, only complicates and distracts from the real issue at hand, the upcoming triumph of tyranny on Earth.

What follows is not "conspiracy theory" but well documented fact. It is not easy to see against the complex background of world affairs. Because of independent media, public awareness of these matters has been increasing in past months. It's a good idea to print out or get hardcopy when appropriate, because very resourceful people are trying hard to stop Internet access to information about these matters.

The New World Order

The predatory globalists are international bankers, not extraterrestrials, but they love only gold, and in their sick insatiable greed, rob all of humanity of the natural right to liberty, earned prosperity, and peace. They do this by manipulating currencies through privately owned central banks like the Federal Reserve Bank of the United States, and with the help of subverted politicians, engineer wars and economic upheaval so that they can lend money to governments for military mobilization and otherwise unnecessary social programs. This is what is meant by "Welfare-Warfare Economies." There is a large detailed body of historical fact about how they have done this for the past two hundred years.

Internationally these people are guilty of crimes against humanity on a scale greater than anyone in all of human history. In their individual countries they are, at very least, guilty of treason. They are allowed to continue in this only because of public ignorance. We can bring these enemies of all human potential to justice with legal precedents like those enacted at Nuremberg, but before an international tribunal can be convened and indictments issued, there must be increased public demand. Liberty-loving people need to learn about these matters and pass it on to others. This in turn must lead to activism: resolutions and petitions by business and civic groups to international organizations, senators, and congressmen.

At this time in history, there is no greater responsibility, and no higher calling. Taking refuge in endless popular modes of escapist delusion will not ensure the future of life and liberty on this planet. Even if adults no longer care about their own futures, they should get involved at least for the sake of the children. In the voting booth, there is merely the illusion of a choice between two NWO puppets. The only real choice is between World Libertarianism and ongoing "two-party" elections geared to globalist tyranny.

The US National debt is nearly twenty trillion dollars, every penny created by fiat counterfeiting. Nobody earned this money. Other nations will follow the US example when it works. All America needs to do is nationalize the Federal Reserve, repudiate the national debt, and demand reparations from the creditors for the amount already swindled from the American people.

Shadow Government
Trading Your Liberty For Our Security

The Enemies of Liberty

Prosperity and peace will follow naturally from worldwide liberty. The enemies of this process are those whose efforts, or lack thereof, put them in opposition to the triumph of Libertarian policies that will bring the closest thing to utopia possible on Earth.

Usually the *intent* of these individuals is much narrower, with little thought given to the bigger picture. The most common goals are the personal attainment of wealth, power, fame, prestige, recognition, acceptance, or stability.

Most are not seeking the deliberate ruination of humanity. Unfortunately the truly powerful people who actually control the world *are* seeking precisely that, and thus far have been extremely successful. World history since 1913 is entirely a product of their machinations.

In this volume we are going to look and a great many categories of people who stand in the way of total excellence in human manifestation. Often a person will be in more than one category, and within these, more than one subcategory as follows, those who are:

Paid For
People given perks or campaign contributions for implementing policy or failing to stress certain areas of truth in their rhetoric. Most of this is legal, but because of the complexity of events, remains *hidden in plain view*.

Status Quo Beneficiaries
These are exploitative elements, along for the ride. Most are worldly syndical people, and this usually involves a high paying position that would otherwise not exist in an honestly run society. Sometimes it involves huge volume manufacture and distribution of product that would otherwise be utilized on a much smaller scale in an honestly run society.

Ideologue
These are the indoctrinated idealists, ignorant intellectually, with an unlimited capacity to rationalize any and all means to the attainment of their ideals. They always defend these as "short-term necessary evils" no matter how destructive or unjust. They don't have a clue as to the real consequences for humanity of the concealed agenda of those who utilize them.

Moral Capability

In humans, he cerebral cortex is the seat of higher moral deliberation. The ability to conceptualize morally is a genetically determined brain skill just like mathematical or mechanical ability. Someone born with effectively no ability to empathize with other living creatures, is what we call a moral moron, or *constitutional psychopath*. They are four percent of the population, one in twenty-five people, and are found in every walk of life.

As with any dichotomy, there is a proportional number of people at the upper end of the moral continuum. Those who are average in the moral sense cluster around the center point

Today, the word *sociopath* is often used as a substitute term for psychopath, but actually denotes two sub-categories:

Psychopath – One vs. Humanity

Dissocial Reaction – One + Family vs. Humanity

This is because the word *psychopath*, in popular use, has come to evoke the image of a violent, wild-eyed individual, with hair-trigger rage reactions. Most of them, however, lead quiet lives of shallow superficial respectability, because they learn early in life that keeping out of trouble is more enjoyable than getting into trouble. Their goals are usually the same as anybody else, but often the means to attainment are very different.

There are many good examples of this among individuals who grow tired of their spouse in a situation where money is involved. The spouse may miss their daily insulin injection, fall down the front staircase, or suffer from a car with leaky brake fluid.

Psychopathy can interact with other behavioral disorders. Criminals are almost always, at very least, constitutional psychopaths. The worst are rapists, snuff and child porn video makes, kidnappers, pedophiles, and those who torture and kill for pleasure. These people are irredeemably evil, and cannot be rehabilitated. The moral integrity and safety of human societies depends upon eliminating them.

Group Psychopathy
There are many factors which determine human behavior, but if one group of people is forty IQ points lower than another group, then it will also be forty moral IQ points lower. If this leads to the taking for granted and general acceptance of certain types of evil behavior, then a tendency for this will be passed along genetically in that group, leading to what is often referred to as a *race of psychopaths*.

Twits will refer to the mature understanding of these matters as *racism*, but tepid knee jerk reactions, after all, is what makes them twits.

IMF Bankers

Most of the big problems on Earth are caused by International Monetary Fund bankers who, via member central banks, manipulate currencies, and with the help of subverted politicians, engineer wars and economic upheaval so they can lend money to governments for military mobilization and otherwise unnecessary social programs.

Globalism, New World Order, is simply the one world government that will allow the IMF banks to have total finance monopoly, e.g. forty percent mortgages, sixty percent refinance.

Countries do not need to borrow from IMF banks, but can have their own central bank and control their own currency. Populations are kept from the knowledge of this by cooperating subverted mainstream media, and by the subverted politicians who keep IMF control in place by voting for it in legislatures.

All that is necessary to have enduring liberty, prosperity, and peace on Earth is to have all counties leave the IMF, set up their own central banks, and tie the amount and value of currency to receipted hours of labor, or a mixed store of scarce and durable commodity.

People of all political parties worldwide must declare that they will not endorse any candidate who doesn't have a detailed plan in hand to get their country out of the IMF, and to nationalize their central bank.

The goal of the Nationalist Revolution novels is to help inspire total worldwide resistance at every level to globalization.

It would be wonderful if we could end world tyranny democratically, but that isn't going to happen. Many will die, but if we don't fight, we will soon have the "cashless society" with national I.D. debit cards, then silicone chip body implants. This will be followed by behavior modification implants, and finally, when they figure out how to do it, a physical matrix for everyone but themselves.

Evil exists. A globalist banker or media boss is a human with the soul of a black widow spider. They cannot be reasoned with, only stopped. We can and will defeat them, but only through heroic action, not with secretly held opinions. The only good globalist is a nonexistent globalist. Free indigenous peoples and cultures will never be safe until they are just an unpleasant memory.

Welfare-Warfare Economy

This is not an anecdotal term. It is the IMF
way-of-things at this time, and will remain so until we
demand something better either in the voting booth or at
gunpoint. Ball games and virtual reality heroism will not
accomplish this.

Welfare
A humane society will provide sustenance for those with a
history of productivity who have incurred legitimate disability.
With healthy economies there will jobs for everyone on Earth
who are able and *willing* to work.

Because of ongoing bad economies, there
has arisen a permanent underclass of people who feel
"entitled" to endless sustenance by government. They
oppose anyone who works for a healthy economy. Those
who engage in violent demonstrations are the modern
counterpart to the Bolshevists who murdered sixty-six million
people in Europe.

Warfare
War and terrorism today are a very difficult study. Just when
you think you understand an event, new information surfaces
showing that it was actually a false flag, usually involving
Globalist traitors in your own government working with
foreign operatives.

The purpose of endless wars is to generate "refugees,"
aided by the EU and UN, to invade countries and destroy
indigenous race and culture everywhere, so that people
lacking identity will except one world government.

Terrorism is supported by deep state funding, open borders,
and police stand-downs. The purpose is to make our daily
lives seem

so dangerous that we will gladly surrender our guns and liberty just to feel "safe." History has shown that the worst enemy people have turns out to be their own government when it gains too much power. Citizen ownership of guns simply represents a balance of power.

Good people need to become proactive about building a better future. We will be rid of these problems only when the Globalists, their subservient minions, and invading outland hoards have been permanently vanquished.

Military-Industrial Complex

This term also, is not anecdotal. All countries must have defensive weapons in place. In a Libertarian Nationalist world, however, the daily function will be only to maintain readiness, not to sustain endless military engagement for the profit of avaricious bankers.

Military Profiteers
Usually these are Globalist agenda-driven elements working for the longer term profits that would come from global finance monopoly,
"Soldiers of Fortune" in the truest sense.

Industrial Profiteers
These are the industrialists who manufacture the machinery of war. In a Libertarian world, they will simply need to retool for farming and space colonization. The good ones will be more than delighted to be able to do this.

In the councils of government, we must guard against the acquisition of unwarranted influence, whether sought or unsought, by the military-industrial complex. The potential for the disastrous rise of misplaced power exists and will persist. ~ Dwight D. Eisenhower 1061

Subverted Politicians

Globalist bankers keep politicians loyal with campaign contributions and easy access to big loans. They create prestigious organizations to teach and implement their agenda. Among these are the United Nations, European Union, Trilateral Commission, Council on Foreign Relations, National Education Association, National Council of Churches.

Politicians, high military officials, prominent industrialists, and media moguls are invited to join these organizations. All this, combined with entrenched subverted government, *deep state*, is correctly called the E*stablishment*.

Subverted Media

IFM bankers have created and subsidized popular media outlets which present or stress information or disinformation which supports their objectives. This usually involves trying to make the public believe that pro Globalist sentiments are already held by a majority of people, and that one will be badly out-of-step if they do not embrace these ideas themselves.

Operation Mockingbird
In the early 1950s, Globalist elements in the Central Intelligence Agency compiled a list of phrases which they felt would elicit knee-jerk responses in the general population. They approached IMF-friendly elements in the mainstream media and persuaded them to cooperate in engineering popular consent for one world government.

It was suggested by the CIA that their phrases be used glibly in a very matter-of-fact way as part of normal daily reportage. The most important of these is *conspiracy theory*.

The CIA knew that lazy apathetic thinkers (almost everybody) would jump on a phrase like this, as an easy-out for rationalizing their own ignorance. e.g. If they don't know

about something complex or hidden, it *must* be only
theoretical, and the person propounding it must, of course,
be *paranoid*, another term on the CIA list. Now the twits can
get back to the ballgame.

Subverted Educators

Charlotte Thomson Iserbyt, former Senior Policy Advisor for
the U.S. Department of Education, disclosed government
policies hidden from the public in her famous book,
The Deliberate Dumbing Down of America.
It was on the New York Times Bestseller List for weeks in
the 1980s, but has anything changed?

Today, schools mix truth with outright lies. If anyone
questions anything, they are labelled *haters.* Good examples
include:

Competition is Cruel
We are all *so* special.
It's insensitive and unfair that anyone ever be graded for the
actual level of their performance in anything. Where is our
sensitivity?

Gender Fluidity
There are many more than two genders.
Scientific research clearly showing that sexual aberration is
a function of genetic mutation, hormone imbalance, or a
mistaken learning process, is really just the bigoted
intolerance of what are simply normal human differences.

Some schools today have small children socialize intimately
with transgender men.
Drag Queen Story Hour. Parents, wake up!

Monoculture is Best
Race is merely a social construct.
Breed up quick, so we can all be the same.

The tedious gray slavery of global monoculture is far more hip and open minded.

The Globalists insure that all these culturally destructive ideas are taught, by giving endowments to schools and colleges, with campaign donations and other payoffs to cooperating legislators.

Globalist accomplices within the education system are usually ideologue twits, many of whom are also entitlement parasites, drug addicts, sex perverts, or invading outlanders. Some are more than one of these. People can only teach with passion from the standpoint of what they are.

Subverted Citizens

Compromised Adults
This is Jean and Joe Six-Pack, couch potato air-heads. They like their ballgames and beer, but never read. They watch only fake news. They never think beyond the end of their own noses, or more than three weeks ahead. A viable future for children, life on Earth one hundred years from today, the evolutionary destiny of mankind, are concepts totally alien to them. Those who do care about these things are seen as trouble-makers.

Misdirected Youth
These are the children ruined intellectually and psycho-sexually by the subverted education system and media. They grow up to be brain dead self-haters.

Reparations Parasites

This usually involves those seeking indemnity for events that happened long ago. Two good examples of this are claimants connected with slavery in the United States, and with what is termed the "holocaust" in WWII Germany.

Falsified History

Sometimes popularly accepted history contains mistakes or exaggerations about events, numbers, motives, or responsibility. At other times outright lies are propounded deliberately.

America

There is an ongoing myth that everybody who were not slaves profited from slavery. In actuality, everybody but the plantation owners, were hurt by slavery, because it eliminated fair completion for the commodities produced, and for jobs in the labor market.

Only two percent of the Caucasian population were slave owners, and this was before the huge influx from Europe after 1850. Today, however, some are asserting that Caucasians, as a group, owe reparations to all descendants of slaves, as a group.

Tell this to Caucasians who lost family fighting to end slavery in the Civil War.

Germany

The six million "holocaust" death toll number was suggested by a magistrate from Vermont who sat at Nuremberg. The IMF-friendly media jumped on this number, and have never let go. There are a few problems, however:

The World Almanac uses official census data.
For 1940, it reports a world Jewish population of 15,319,359.
For 1949, 15,713,638.

Under the terms of the Geneva Convention, the Red Cross inspected all the concentration camps once every two weeks. Their official estimate of the total number who died in all the camps is 271,301. This includes non-Jews.

American forensic doctors examined hundreds of bodies and found only typhus and starvation as the causes of death, not even one death from poison gas.

When the Russians liberated the camps in Poland, including Auschwitz, they did not allow the press into the camps for five years. When they finally removed the restriction, journalists got to photograph all those gas chambers that nobody remembers seeing who visited the camps during the war years.

IMF bankers, of course, continue to lend money to Germany for the ongoing reparations to Israel based on the six million estimate. Anyone who speaks up is shouted down as a *Holocaust denier.*

Self-Disabling Parasites

These are people who are perfectly able to work, but who use subterfuge to keep from doing so. There are several categories. Some may be in more than one:

Breeders
These are welfare mothers who have eight children while being completely subsidized by government. These are men who brag on the city bus about fathering seventeen illegitimate children. Condoning either is like poising the public water supply.

Wastrels
These are people who find every way possible to keep from working. They include borrowers, gamblers, gigolos, moochers.

Mental Cases
With the exception of aberration having physical origin, the clinical catalogue of dysfunctional behavior is really just a list of the different types of bad moral character.

A good example is the neurotic who develops
a *phobia for work* as a reaction to some unrelated incident in
youth. Morally ambivalent psychiatrists are often complicit in
sustaining this, because they know that loving parents want
the young person to take whatever amount of time is
necessary to *work through* the problem. There are endless
sessions, but very few cures.

Drug Addicts
The moral maturity of a person at the time they begin using a
psychotropic drug remains fixed, until they stop using the
drug. This includes anti-depressants and tranquilizers
prescribed by doctors who receive a manufacturer
commission for every prescription.

Today many users start on drugs at an early age. Good
business people don't want an adult worker with the
maturely of an eight-year-old. Additionally, drug use often
interferes with motivation, attention span, and coordination.

Sex Perverts
Colleges today host an endless freak show of transgender
monstrosities. There is usually euphemistic terminology for
this, like the very computeresque *non binary*. Those who
sport these labels believe that they are intellectual pioneers
in a brave new world of greater tolerance and expanded
consciousness.

Invaders

Legal
These are immigrants whose influx into any country
ultimately destroys the race and culture of the indigenous
population. Their immigration is legal, but would not be, if the
country were not subverted to the purposes of Globalism. In
the interest of racial preservation, this problem must be
addressed immediately worldwide by any means available.

Illegal Individuals

Many of the gatecrashers who violate borders come back no matter how many times they are deported. There are instances of some who have returned over fifty times. If they knew that they would be executed immediately upon return, most would probably not return.

Illegal Hordes

At this writing (5/26/2019), there is an ongoing invasion across the southern border of the United States. It would be perfectly appropriate to use loudspeakers to warn the invaders, and then at intervals with fighter planes, strafe with machine fire, those who ignore the warning. If a sovereign nation is to remain free, it must enforce its borders.

Who's Who

In 1933, Friedreich Nietzsche propounded the ideal of the Ubermensch, or Superman. This does not involve supernaturalism or anything unattainable, but as a concept has been misunderstood, joked down, and twisted by cowards and lowlifes ever since.

The superman (men and women) are simply people who do not have to victimize or encroach upon others to survive in a free society. They transcend the myths and false moralities of everyday experience, and work in some area of magnificent obsession to make the world a better place. They are here among us, not to be stoned, cool and jazzy, but to save the day.

The subhuman is the opposite of this, people who have no capacity except to encroach upon others in a free society. This is primarily a function of low I.Q. Their intrinsic inferiority puts them in opposition to social policies that will lead to liberty, prosperity, and peace. They are essentially enemies of evolutionary destiny. If evolved humanity is to survive, then the subhuman must be eliminated. The easiest, most humane, and best way is through mass sterilization.

In terms of the narrative at hand, the superman is the Libertarian Nationalist warrior who will oppose Globalism even unto death. The subhuman is any of the people listed herein as enemies of liberty. When they are gone, good people will rest briefly, then the Golden Age of Humanity will begin.

Strategies

Apathetic Non Resistance
This is not a viable option. In the long term, globalization would do more damage to life on Earth than a full nuclear exchange between all nations. Doing nothing about the Globalists can lead only to one or the other.

Liberian Nationalist Revolution
A reformatted after-the-fact story version of the following section appears at the end of every novel in the series. Read on, and see why.

Libertarian Nationalist Revolution

Most of the big problems on Earth are caused by parasitic international bankers who, via central banks, manipulate currencies, and with the help of subverted politicians, engineer wars and economic upheaval so that they can lend money to governments for military mobilization and otherwise unnecessary social programs.

The Shadow Government / New World Order agenda, called Globalization, is merely Totalitarian Socialism with One World Government, giving absolute monopoly to predatory bankers. Any reputable economist will tell you that what the World Libertarian Order proposes will result in ongoing liberty, prosperity, and peace for all people on Earth. Saving the world is a big job, but it's the best, and involves the making right of all past mistakes, not mere adaptation to the aftermath. No single group, governmental body, or army is expected to affect this entire program. Those who like the future vision depicted, should simply do whatever they can towards the desired end.

Without the Globalists, we will have a future for the entire world, free of economic upheaval, war, and pollution, with no encroachment on any living thing, indigenous peoples enjoying strict population control, race and culture preservation, absolute individual liberty, prosperity, and peace as separate sovereign nations competing in a free world market.

Following is a ten point program, which must be implemented to liberate societies so that natural order can prevail. The best approach will vary from one country to another because of what has occurred in the past, but the variations involve only short term emphasis and sequence, not policy or principles. The time frame for phasing in any particular policy must be of sufficient duration for smooth transition tp minimize any short term bad effects upon individuals or economies.

This is a summary, and may suggest the need for further reading, so please press ahead.

Ten Steps to Libertarian Nationalist Revolution

1. Revolution

Politicians:

All at the same time, stand up and be courageous. Show some integrity. Stop serving the New World Order parasites. Accept the premise that government is at best a necessary evil and that the less of it we have, the better. Please support all measures outlined herein.

Everybody Else:

Initiate revolution. Support all popular measures that are in a basic Libertarian direction, such as budget balancing. When there is no other choice, deal with gross encroachments against individual liberty covertly on an individual basis. Educate the upcoming generation at the grass roots level, about the sole workability of Libertarian principles so that un-Libertarian elements can finally be voted out of office everywhere. Maintain health, practice martial skills, and stay well-armed in case we get a chance to do it sooner. All this is the only difficult part. The rest is simple and could then be implemented quickly unless otherwise specified.

2. Banking and Trade

In every country, nationalize privately owned central banks, like the US Federal Reserve, repudiate the national debt, and demand reparations for the amount already swindled by the creditors, as a civil alternative to being put on trial for engineering every war and ruined economy over the past two hundred years, or being the beneficiary heirs thereto, all of which is easily provable from existing historical records. Return to currencies backed by durable commodity of intrinsic value, like gold or a mixed store of precious metals, the value of which will be determined in the world marketplace.

Consumers worldwide will have total product choice. Goods offered in the free world market will be produced solely within each country by the citizens of that country, with no foreign ownership of business anywhere. Banks will lend only within their own countries. Once all nations are prospering, few will think it good practice to invest away from home, and imbalances will subside. Simultaneously, phase out all subsidies and unjust regulation of business, trade, financial transfers, and banks.

For any bank, including the central bank, to maintain less than a one hundred percent reserve at all times is simply dishonest. The new policies will correct things easily with mandatory disclosure to depositors about actual amounts held in reserve, and clear information on what it all means.

3. Taxation

Eliminate wealth redistribution at gunpoint, aka taxes, and institute specific user fees and designated lotteries. This will not happen simultaneously in all areas of spending, but

immediately wherever possible. From here forward
unnecessary foreign adventures by governments will have to
be paid for only by those who support them.

 4. War

In this new scenario, war will fast become just an unhappy
memory. The energies previously squandered in these
conflicts will be channeled into undersea farming, renewable
energy technology, space exploration, and interplanetary
mining operations. Defense spending everywhere can be cut
to a safe minimum, substituting standing military with a
skeleton crew of officers for the coordination of a voluntary
citizen militia adequate to any emergency. To this end,
replace frivolous athletics in the schools with basic martial
and survival training.

5. Socialism

End the artificial sustenance of non-viability. Gradually
phase out social programs and entitlements as the improving
economy and rate of employment makes this possible in
each particular locality. This will be done slowly enough so
that nobody will be hurt. How quickly this can happen,
however, will be a great surprise to most people. Nobody will
be hungry in a Libertarian society. There will be an
emergency fund to alleviate desperation caused by
unpredictable local catastrophe or incurred disability. This
can be funded by designated lotteries at the federal and
state level.

6. Crime

Deal intelligently with crime:

- Legalize victimless crimes involving consensual areas of
human contract. Free all those confined for victimless crimes
with a public apology, a little money to tide them over, and a
list of realistic job offers.

- Recognize the true bad guys: rapists, human traffickers, kidnappers, child molesters, child and snuff porn filmmakers, arbitrary murderers, and serial killers. These people are irredeemable constitutional psychopaths who have made an unforgivable breech with humanity. For the safety and moral integrity of societies they must be put painlessly to death. Opponents of this should appreciate that one needn't be a rocket scientist to figure out that all it takes to avoid being executed for these terrible things is simply not to do them.

- Replace prisons with self-sustaining isolation communities, several square miles with agriculture, livestock, and small manufacturing. As economies improve, the inevitable one percent of humanity simply unable to support themselves can be offered permanent sustenance by private charity as per specified terms, such as voluntary sterilization. Any such individuals refusing this option will have to shift for themselves. If this causes them to make encroachment on anyone else's liberty, they will be placed in isolation communities.

7. Protectionism

As the distortions produced by hundreds of years of unnatural coercive government slowly begin to subside, cautiously phase out all unnecessary or unjust protectionist measures such as unnecessary safety regulations.

8. Education

Institute programs in schools to teach children about what went wrong in the past and how Libertarian policies have improved everything. Explain the manipulative relationship that previously existed between international finance and politicians. Supplement this with rigorous teaching about devolving humanity, racial preservation, excess birth rates, birth control, disease, and all individual classes of drugs. Make understanding of all this requisite for promotion. Teach the truth for forty years before eliminating public education.

9. Adjustments

Make all adjustments associated with simple Libertarian decency and smart living.
Examples include:

- Stop unnecessary environmental pollution as soon as this is viable. No pay-offs for ten year "feasibility" studies or twenty year "implementation" programs. Just stop it.

- Institute requirements in livestock production, zoo administration, and pet ownership based upon humane, free-range, hormone/drug-free models.

- Stop the cruel decadent down breeding of pets into evolutionary non-viability. Sterilize the existing animals. Ask yourself why little dogs are so nervous and angry that they bark viciously all day, every day. Would you not be angry if captors had done this to you?

- Give national park and forest lands back to the native populations from whom they were originally stolen. This with the provision that they continue to run the lands at a high standard, for the enjoyment of all. Current non-native employees can be offered life tenure or a new job.

- Overhaul medicine, stressing nutritional solutions, both therapeutic and preventive, as opposed to only pharmacological and surgical options. Eliminate the duplicitous role of the physician as both personal doctor and commission salesman for drug companies, Allow doctors to prescribe only within generic categories, the specific choice of drugs being left to the patients who select for themselves on the basis of price and manufacturer reputation.

- Respect the right of individuals to decide when their life is no longer viable. Establish regional centers where people can be put into cryonic suspension, or receive a lethal injection and be cremated.

10. Population and Race

Deal decisively with the issues of population and race:

- History shows that smaller numbers of people in any given place work best, so long as there are enough to defend the borders. For the land mass of Earth, the *ideal* population is 320 million people. This number was passed c 900 A.D. By the word *ideal* we mean a level consistent with vital self-actualization and opulent joy in living, rather than mere subsistence in anguished mediocrity. To this end, rigidly enforce a limit of two children per couple. More than two is an unjust encroachment upon others, like house burglary. World population will slowly decline to workable levels everywhere. The projected ideal numbers are as follows:

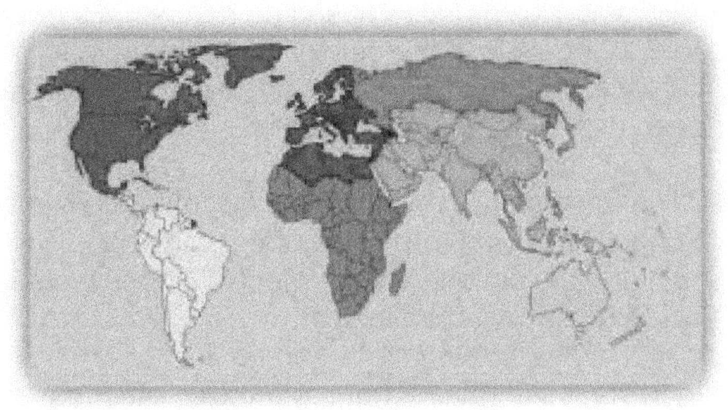

Canada, United States, Mexico
50,000,000

Central, South America
50,000,000

Greenland, Europe, Northern Africa
50,000,000

Southern Africa
50,000,000

Russia
50,000,000

Near, Middle East, Asia
50,000,000

Australia, New Zealand
20,000,000

- Workable societies must be based on natural principals. It is natural for people to feel most comfortable among those of their own race and ethnicity. In all of human history there has never been a multiracial or multicultural society which did not self-destruct because of the unnatural mixing. The New World Order bankers, who work for totalitarian Socialism and world monoculture, want everyone to mix together, so they can lend money to national governments who must deal with all the resulting social problems.

- All people have the natural right to grow up among their own racial kinsmen. Resident racial outlanders are simply an unjust encroachment upon the personal liberty of indigenous peoples. To survive, we must emphasize race preservation and the prevention of global monoculture. Interracial marriage advocates are attempting to eliminate all existing races. They try to sound very interested in human variety, but their breed-up quick programs, long term, will completely obliterate human variety by making what are now separate races into one race. Variety is the spice of life. Imagine the tedium of universal sameness. The globalist bankers want to destroy race and culture. They know that one world government, giving global finance monopoly, will be more acceptable to people with no racial or ethnic identity.

- A common falsehood perpetrated by politicians in service to big business seeking cheap labor has been that ongoing immigration is necessary to keep industry alive. In actuality, business simply expands to accommodate any available work force. With worldwide prosperity, people will not flee their ancestral homelands.

- Note that third-world people usually favor globalization because it will allow them to prosper via social programs paid for by productive host populations. The predatory bankers know that countries with hordes of immigrant third-worlders, if the globalization question comes to a ballot referendum, will be far more likely to relinquish sovereignty.

- Close borders everywhere to immigrants of non-indigenous race. Anybody can leave, and a great many will begin to return home. Request voluntary sterilization of all who choose to remain in host countries, with special retirement programs for those who cooperate and adoption priorities for qualified couples within this category. No restrictions on travel. Tourists from now on will be able to enjoy the full undiluted potency of indigenous cultures everywhere.

- There will be new technology for determining constitutional psychopathy, even in the prenatal state, along with intrauterine diagnosis of fetal deformity, mental retardation, and genetic predisposition to sexual perversion. This will lead to the elimination of human non-viability everywhere on earth.

- Implement an equitable solution for the problems caused by a century of Socialism in unnaturally increasing the quantity, while undermining the quality, of people everywhere. There will be new foolproof brain-scan methods for determining intelligence. Use it to assess IQ in populations worldwide. Request voluntary sterilization of all those having an IQ of 94 or less, also with special retirement benefits and adoption priorities. Because higher moral conceptualization is a function of the cerebral cortex, these IQ adjustments, along with the elimination of constitutional psychopathy, will effectively spell an end to commonplace moral stupidity on this planet.

A Brighter Future

When all nations have attained free enterprise with global free trade, a basically Libertarian world will finally have been achieved. Evil will still exist on Earth at interpersonal levels, but it will no longer rule the day, nor will it never again be institutionalized by governments.

Dumbing Down of Populations

Under the influence and tutelage attached to Globalist banker endowments for education, American schools have been dumbing kids down for over 100 years.

The goal is to replace logical common sense reactions to life with moral lassitude. This is done by slowly changing the curriculum with false ideas about wealth, economics, science, health, nutrition, sex, gender, natural selection, archaeology, race, history, good, evil, right, wrong, love, hate, spirituality, liberty, security, and national sovereignty. This is done, not just with false emphasis and interpretation, but often using outright falsehood.

After graduation, the dumbing down continues, especially with selective information about current events, from the subverted media. The upside-down agenda we see today is to make reality and policy conform to a distorted world view instead of changing the world view and policy to be in conformity with workable reality.

Under Libertarian policies, with increasing prosperity and the return of indigenous peoples to their ancestral homelands, there will be a resurgence of ethnic and cultural pride everywhere. We will see it in the arts, music, and culinary industries. Tourism will be up worldwide. Travelers will enjoy the full potency of other people's indigenous cultures everywhere on earth.

People will be comfortable with who and what they are. All the phony *gender fluidity* nonsense will be a thing of the past. The bleaching and dying of hair and skin in mimicry of other races, will be gone, and there will be no more retarded catcalls of *racism* or *phobia* for every nuance of normal human preference.

Footnote: Gender Fluidity

There are two biological genders. Appearances to the contrary come from five sources: random genetic mutation, inherited genetic predisposition, hormone imbalance, mistakes in leaning as outlined by Sigmund Freud, and outright perversion usually associated with drug augmented aberration and the false belief that every random impulse must be nurtured for the true liberation of the evolved self.

Gender is fixed, but gender-specific behavior is variable. A puritanical view is that gender specific behavior is fixed, therefore gender must be variable. At first, this might seem arbitrary, but on closer view, the utility is that it absolves people of responsibility for their actions. In this way they can blame dysfunctional behavior on random genetic chance and avoid any proactive effort towards constructive change.

Suggested Reading - The Globalist Agenda:

How the Elite Control your mind and Your Life

Education & History
Research for Yourself...

The Deliberate Dumbing Down of America
by Charlotte Thomson Iserbyt

Charlotte Thomson Iserbyt, former Senior Policy Advisor in the U.S. Department of Education, blew the whistle in the `80s on government activities withheld from the public. Her inside knowledge will help you protect your children from controversial methods and programs. Visit author's website and buy a hardcopy of the book.

Underground History of American Education
by John Taylor Gatto

As John Taylor Gatto explains the secret of American
schooling is that it doesn't teach the way children learn, and
it isn't supposed to. It took seven years of reading and
reflection to finally figure out that mass schooling of the
young by force was a creation of the four great coal powers
of the nineteenth century. Nearly one hundred years later, on
April 11, 1933, Max Mason, president of the Rockefeller
Foundation, announced to insiders that a comprehensive
national program was underway to allow, in Masonic words,
"the control of human behavior."

Who Controls Our Children?

While parents, schools, provinces and states across North
America bicker about the democratic process of running
public schools, forces are manipulating education from
behind the scenes. Major international players are reshaping
public education to suit their own self-serving agendas,
without regard for the wants of parents and the welfare of
their children. This video lecture by Peg Luksik documents
how today's educational system dumb down kids
deliberately, making zombie-like people who don't ask any
questions but just follow orders. Also see her book "Outcome
Based Education: The State's Assault on Our Children's
Values."

America BC
by Barry Fell

Barry Fell's book on ancient settlers in the new world
prior to Columbus.

Forbidden Archeology
by Michael A. Cremo and Richard L. Thompson

Over the past two centuries researchers have found bones
and artifacts showing that people like ourselves existed on
earth millions of years ago. But the scientific establishment
has ignored these remarkable facts because they contradict
the dominant views of human origins and antiquity. Cremo
and Thompson challenge us to rethink our understanding of
human origins, identity, and destiny. Forbidden Archeology
takes on one of the most fundamental components of the
modern scientific world view, and invites us to take a
courageous first step towards a new perspective.

Brain Washing 101

Brainwashing 101 is a provocative short documentary (46
minutes) showing how university faculty and administrators
use tools such as "speech codes" to force their political
views upon students. In this cutting expose, documentary
filmmakers Maloney, Browning, and Greenberg shine a light
on political correctness, academic bias, student censorship,
even administrative cover-ups of death threats, at three
schools: Bucknell University, the University of Tennessee at
Knoxville, and California Polytechnic State University
(Cal Poly).

It's OK to be of Any Race

Wake up! This includes being white. Today, those of other races are saying that white people are bad because, in recent memory, they colonized other peoples. Throughout history every race has tried to colonize other people. The anger comes only from jealousy. Whites have simply been more successful at it.

Let us also notice that those who criticize whites in the universities, almost to an individual, mimic whites in every way possible They bleach their skin, dye their hair, cultivate patterns of dress, speech, and mannerisms, all in the image of the thing they claim to hate so much, but can never be, genetically.

Today, members of races who chose to quarrel, dance around cook fires, and mutter incantations for twelve thousand years, while Europeans and Orientals were building civilizations, now seem to think that they have an intrinsic right to breed their way into more advanced civilizations. They seek to upgrade their own family genetically, while ruining the gene pool of the victim culture. All this in the name of "social justice."

So, here I am, Dr. C. M. Zimbobo, back home, thinking of a white girl in the USA, who sat in front of me in my genetics class at a state university I will not name. I cannot easily get her out of my mind, but will eventually. I choose not to rape, or to infiltrate another race. This is because I am a *man*, and I know that my people have equal potential to evolve, and become what white people in general, and a few exceptional others like myself, are now.

Diversity Delusion / Fake Racism

Belief in multiculturalism is always sustained by members of an inferior culture who want to live parasitically at the expense of a superior culture. They fabricate ideas about racism, and drug themselves into disability, so as to be sustained by government. They think of themselves as "good" people, too depressed by "racism" to work, the "disenfranchised" victims of all those "haters."

Real life tells a different story. It is our natural evolutionary heritage from millennia of fierce tribal competition for food and shelter, to prefer the company of our own racial kinsmen. What the parasites call "racism" is simply a natural human reaction to other races.

Any form of government not based upon natural principles is doomed to failure from the outset. There is no example in all of human history of any multicultural society that did not self-destruct because of the multiculturalism. It is also natural, however, to be peace-loving in a non-self-destructive way towards peoples of other lands, to visit them as travelers and enjoy the full undiluted potency of their cultures.

Human parasites propound the false idea that race mixing constitutes "diversity." If races mix, in two hundred years, where is the diversity? Real diversity is ongoing indigenous populations in separate sovereign nations competing in a free world market. Variety, not the grey slavery of global monoculture, is the spice of life.

The European Union and the United Nations are totally corrupt Globalist minions in service to International Monetary Fund (IMF) bankers. Both organizations are forcing incompatible races into proximity all over the world. Their purpose is not the "brotherhood of Man." IMF money masters work for one world government *only* to gain total finance monopoly and absolute control of everyone on earth.

In the meantime, they profit by lending money to government needed to address the endless problems caused by multiculturalism.

Most main stream media is owned by, or otherwise subverted to, the interests of IMF bankers. In the early 1960s, came Project Mockingbird, now eclassified. Globalist elements in the Central Intelligence Agency approached IMF subverted media with a list of words and phrases they contrived to help engineer consent for one world government by eliciting knee-jerk reactions in the intellectually lazy majority. Examples include:

bigotry, conspiracy theory, paranoia
provincialism, small town thinking, subtle racism
white male, white privilege, white supremacy

Since 1947, the covert posture of the Globalists towards the youth of the world has been "Dope 'em up and dumb 'em down." They have been very successful. Cognitive dissonance abounds. Today, sullen drug addicted self-haters work for the destruction of all races and cultures, especially their own, while shouting the catcall of "racist" against any who work for the preservation of all races and cultures. Breed-up-quick advocates never look more than a few weeks ahead. They never contemplate ideas like *evolutionary destiny*. Twits will throw down all human potential forever, just to be fashionably liberal minded sounding at campus drug parties.

When all nations leave the IMF and nationalize their central banks, there will be prosperity everywhere on Earth. There will be no economic oppression to run away from. Countries of origin will be able to accept the return of those who wish live once again in their rightful ancestral homelands. When this splendid day comes, there will be no further excuse for the delusions of multiculturalism.

Fallacy of Critical Race Theory

Critical Race Theory is simply racial envy directed against people of European ancestry, but calling itself insightful historical analysis, a pseudo intellectual posturing that "subtle racism" has become institutionalized systemically in the way that multicultural countries are organized.

Underlying false premises include:

That multiculturalism is a workable way to run human societies. There are no historical examples to support this idea.

That low IQ populations on average are equal morally to high IQ populations. Since the cerebral cortex is the seat of higher moral deliberation in humans, on average, a low

IQ group is a also low Moral IQ group.

That less highly evolved racial outlanders should be allowed to reside in countries occupied by more highly evolved people.

That the preference to be among one's own racial kinsmen is not natural, but learned "racism" based on "ignorance."

That the inability of less highly evolved people to compete successfully in a free society is the result of some kind of underlying foul play, rather than a simple lack of natural ability, and that the more highly evolved people should be robbed institutionally to upgrade the living standard of those less capable.

All of this has only given increase among low IQ peoples to a psychology of wrongful blaming and unwarranted entitlement.

In America, for a long time it was generally held that Caucasians owned Negroes a debt because of slavery. This led to destructive programs like Affirmative Action.

Eventually it was realized that less than one percent of Caucasians in America are descended from slave owners, who were the only people who profited from slavery. Everyone else, including Caucasians, were hurt by slavery because of the effect on crop prices and the job market.

Once these facts came to light, a new body of untruth calling itself social justice had to be created to falsely justify the ongoing undeserved government benefit programs for slack-jawed outlanders with no work ethic.

Today, under Critical Race Theory, white people are being blamed for every normal consequence accruing to the gap between themselves and less highly evolved races.

But… if countries everywhere get their central banks out of the International Monetary Fund and issue their own national currencies there will be ongoing worldwide prosperity for everyone willing to work. When this happens, countries of origin will be able to accept the return of their displaced racial kinsmen. What follows will be the Golden Age of Mankind.

Worldwide Racial Displacement

Intelligent Humanity is an Endangered Species

Evolutionary destiny is the imperative for the unimpeded, ever-more varied and complex expression of intelligence. The mechanism for this is natural selection, the principle that organisms manifesting traits having negative survival value, will reproduce at a lesser rate because they will not live long enough to do so. This will ultimately cause the trait to die out in that species, unless those manifesting the traits are given unnatural sustenance to prolong their lives and periods of reproduction.

When non self-sustaining organisms are sustained artificially and end up reproducing when they would otherwise have not, evolution stops and devolution begins. Devolution is the reverse of evolution. The damage to evolutionary destiny is even worse if the evolutionary expression of self-sustaining organisms is encroached upon in the process. These principles apply to all life forms, including humanity.

Evolution will not continue, and ultimately intelligent mankind will not survive, if societies continue to act as subsidized breeding farms for human non-self-sustainability.
Recognition of this does not mean that anybody needs to go hungry or starve. In a Libertarian Republic all people can live long happy lives. Ongoing sustenance of chronically unemployable people can be provided efficiently without

dragging down human excellence using coercive government wealth redistribution. It is also possible with education about birth control to help people to curb the encroachment they make by having more than two children in a world that passed the ideal population of 320 million people in the year 900 A.D..

Race Preservation is Not Injustice

It's perfectly normal to feel more comfortable and at ease among one's own kind. This is an instinctive trait which comes from tens of thousands of years of fierce tribal competition for food and shelter. Nobody should ever allow themselves to be put on the defensive about having these normal feelings. Sometimes normalcy in this regard is mitigated by other things: spirituality, education, fashion, brainwashing, fear, lust, insanity, greed, naivety, social masochism, self-hatred, stupidity, or any combination of these.

It's safe to say that a person's feelings are always based upon the total of what they have experienced. Most so called prejudice is just a normal human reaction to what an individual has experienced. Since we all have different experiences, we all have different reactions.

A stereotype is the random generalization that an individual member of an identifiable group, for better or for worse, possesses a particular characteristic, which may or may not be more common among members of that group, this without any substantive knowledge of the person as an individual. Stereotypes are usually based upon race, nationality, sex, age, and creed.

There is a double standard about constructive racial pride. If a member of a less highly evolved race shows it, he is praised for cultural consciousness, If a member of a more highly evolved race shows it, he is scorned for divisiveness or bigotry.

Dictionary definition: "Racism is the belief that race is the sole determinant of character in the individual". There are very few people who believe anything like this. Everyday experience contradicts it. When people speak the deeper truth about race, however, it's usually shouted down with catcalls about hatred and bigotry. What this tells us is that if we want to be thought of as being loving and open-minded, we have to go along with social lies.

Ideological falsehood about group member potential is always reinforced using induction, that is, reasoning backwards from exceptional particular instances to a false general premise. Individuals must be judged individually. That doesn't mean, however, that we have to be deaf, dumb, and blind as to what is true about groups, or the adverse effect that one group can have upon another when it is wrongfully displaced from its rightful ancestral homeland. What hurts a group, hurts individuals.

Evolved Intelligence is being Lost Forever

Probably the best definition of a race traitor is "one who will throw down everything that has been gained through four and a half billion years of evolution to be fashionably liberal minded sounding at cocktail parties". The differences between racial groups are based on far more than mere physical appearance. More importantly, there are significant differences in intelligence. This has many consequences.

Science shows that the seat of higher moral deliberation is the cerebral cortex. The ability to conceptualize morally is tied to overall intelligence. Less highly evolved races not only have a lower average IQ, but also a lower average moral IQ. This leads to poor relations with other groups. All one needs to do is to search "crime by race" on the Internet. Statistics show these things very clearly. Ivory tower wishful thinkers will, of course, deny, or twist, every nuance of truth in this area.

The interbreeding of a more highly evolved race with one less highly evolved, results in a new race somewhere between the two original races, in humans, usually closer in manifestation to the lower. Once racial interbreeding gets started in any society, devolution and downfall has begun.

It's usually the lower members of the more highly evolved race who interbreed with the upper members of the less highly evolved race. As time passes, more and more intelligence disappears overall, and group differences become increasingly blurred. Those of mixed race usually identify with the lower half of their ancestry out of a need for self-justification, and are usually not accepted by members of the higher race. The most noble thing such a person can do for evolutionary destiny in general, is to identify the higher race, abstain from the gene pool, and adopt children.

The Role of Politics

Ambitious representatives of less highly evolved races will always champion the genetic intermixing of their people with the more highly evolved race. Why wouldn't they? They have everything to gain and nothing to lose.
 Interracial marriage advocates are trying to obliterate race by making all people intp one race. Dominant genetic traits are those which win out over long periods of interbreeding. Examples are brown eyes and black hair. Recessive genetic traits are the ones that lose out. These include light eye colors, such as green, blue, and hazel. Also gone forever will be light hair colors, such as blond, ash, auburn, and red.

If one race possesses mostly recessive genetic traits, then that race will be destroyed by race mixing. Self-respecting members of such a race will quite properly perceive all the breed-up-quick philosophy as a threat to the continued existence of their own race. They will feel that interracial dating websites are not examples of open-mindedness or cultural progress, but only of ignorance and societal decay, something effectively akin to an epidemic of fatal disease.

The real issue is racial preservation, diversity rather than sameness, variety rather than monoculture.

International finance manipulates politicians and always promotes any massive government spending program that will allow them to lend money. This includes ongoing programs that implement unworkable Socialist policies. They escape the cultural impact, because they can afford to live or vacation anywhere on Earth. People have the natural right to grow up in a society among their own racial kinsmen and should not accept being coerced at gunpoint by cruel socialist slave masters into intermixing with sullen, angry racial outlanders, who have an in-your-face attitude and speak with a tone of blaming.

It's important to know that third-world people usually favor globalization, because it will allow them to prosper from social programs paid for by productive host populations. Globalist bankers know that countries with multitudes of immigrant third-worlders, if globalization comes to a ballot referendum, will be far more likely to relinquish sovereignty. This is the reason for all the new indigent faces in productive countries.

Solution: Make the Whole World Free

Science teaches that when two groups compete for the same ecological niche, the stronger will destroy the weaker. Distance between the groups, of course, eliminates the competition. A good non-human example is timber wolves and coyotes. Both are *canis lupus*, but they are also natural enemies. Both survive very nicely if they are at a distance from each other. Coyotes like to travel around a good deal, but the smart ones have learned not go within seventy five miles of timber wolves.

Those who would rob you of your liberty, or threaten the existence or evolutionary destiny of your race, are your mortal enemies. There are two ways to deal with them. You can either have them at a distance or eliminate them completely, at very least by stopping their further reproduction. Which you choose should be determined only by your perception of possibility and cost.

It's normal for the people of a more highly evolved race to take up arms against those who seek to destroy their race, and with it the evolutionary destiny of mankind. There are, however, more peaceful solutions.

Populations displaced by coercion have the natural right to return to their ancestral homelands. This option can be made legal through the cooperation of governments everywhere. Worldwide liberty and capitalism will produce worldwide prosperity. This will allow populations who have been unjustly displaced to return to their ancestral homelands, because the newly prospering nations will be able to easily accommodate their return.

Displaced people of reproducing age who are realistic, responsible, and mature will want to participate in this great adventure. They can entrust their property to older friends and relatives who choose to remain in the host counties. Their property can then be sold at a time advantageous from the standpoint of market.

There is no substitute for the splendid integrity of living in a place where you are wanted, and where you don't have to blame, or thank, anyone but yourself, for how well you do.

Eric F. Magnuson
October 15, 2008
Late Morning

The following is an adaptation of a essay written by Dirk Aubrey Lokison in 1983 about racial displacement problems particular to the United States. In the original version, specific ethnic and racial groups were identified. The WLO's goal is not to hurt anyone's feelings, just to make a better world, so I took these specific references out. The who-does-it is gone, but the what-they-do remains. See if you can ID the various groups. I also made editorial changes for easy readability, but not for meaning or content. Those of European heritage will think of many culturally displaced individuals who they like or love. Personal affiliations, however, must not interfere with more important matters such as race preservation and evolutionary destiny. Goals must be prioritized. We can visit our friends overseas when they are happy and prospering back in their ancestral homelands. - EFM

Displaced Racial Populations in America

People of European ancestry are the founders of America as it is now constituted, and must not be hindered in the establishment of a totally free society by antithetical groups who never belonged here in the first place. There are many specific problems in the USA which accrue to the presence of displaced populations. There is, of course, in every group a percentage of decent people. In the groups that are hurting the United States however:

- Many are significantly less intelligent. Those who question the accuracy of intelligence tests need only look at the long record of almost total non-achievement by certain groups in both America and in their countries of origin. They are often loud, belligerent, and foul-mouthed. Their presence in America spoils the quality of life for people of European heritage.

- Many have out-bred their ability to feed themselves at home. Americans should not have to put up with vast throngs of third-worlders coming into our country to do the same thing here. Most of the invaders are tedious and uninspired, addicted to indiscriminate reproduction and cowardly medieval religion.

- Many are cruel, fanatical, and given to terrorism. The dangerous ones exist in sufficient percentage so that we shouldn't have to worry about which are which.

- Many are conniving monoculturalists who are openly aggressive towards the host populations of European ancestry. This parasitic element sponsored and now exploits the Socialism that is destroying America. We shouldn't have to put up with the vile dispiriting nihilism of these wandering internationalist blood suckers.

- Many are intelligent, quiet, polite, and hard working. There are, however, enough of them in their homelands. In the interest of our own preservation, we should not welcome vast numbers of them here with their cheerless similarity of appearance. It's simply a bad move genetically from the standpoint of human aesthetics and variety.

Social lies are always used by collectivist governments to justify non-viable policies. There are two big lies guiding American social policy. One pertains to who did what. Virtually all black people in the USA are descended from those who were brought to America as slaves. Most white people in America, however, are not descended from greedy southern plantation owners, and have inherited no culpability in any of this. The presence of black people in America is, for most white people, simply an unjust cultural and genetic encroachment. The other big lie is that all free people were unjustly enriched by the institution of slavery. The truth is that the only people who gained from slavery were the plantation owners. Everybody else was hurt because of what it did to the price of commodities and the labor market.

The slavery lies are used to promote so called "social justice" via socialist wealth redistribution. Affirmative Action programs deny education to more qualified people of higher intelligence. Colleges in the United States have been invaded by loud, motor-mouth jokers who disrupt the study of serious students. When anyone asks them to please quiet down, they often respond defiantly with name calling and threats of violence. This is especially true first semester, before many of them flunk out. Anybody who doubts any of this need only sit for a while in any college library of computer lab and listen to what goes on, and then see for themselves who is responsible. Try riding a city bus over time and then ask yourself why ninety nine percent of the trouble consistently comes from twelve percent of the people.

Non-Coercive Solutions

Large percentages within all displaced population groups are antagonistic to the interests of liberty loving Americans of European descent. Only small percentages have demonstrated any real comprehension of free-enterprise principles. Their continued insistence on the injustice of Affirmative Action and unnecessary social programs is the most concrete expression of this.

Admitting the truth of all these things does not mean that anyone should condone cruelty, injustice, or disrespectful behavior towards anyone else. Nor should it be used to refute the great accomplishments of exceptional individuals within any displaced group.

On the average, however, people of European ancestry have everything to lose and nothing to gain through further association with displaced populations. The terrible injustices of history cannot be rectified by the further injustice of perpetuating Socialism in America. Two wrongs don't make a right.

Our greatness as a nation can now only be realized by doing what is clearly most workable. It is in our interest to help displaced people get back home to whatever country they came from. Mass influx should be stopped immediately. Incompatible groups already in the United States must be allowed to return to their countries of origin.

So called "Native" Americans are actually first wave European immigrants who came here via the Alaskan Land Bridge fourteen thousand years ago. They are the only people who truly deserve to be in America, but there are not enough of them left to defend the borders of a country this size. Most of them are gone because of diseases brought by later European settlers. As Americans we owe the survivors a great deal.

We should give Native Americans back good tracts of government land to inhabit, plus all of the National Parks and

Forests, to be run by them for the use of all Americans. Their religion is much like the original spirituality of Europeans. Whenever possible they should be given the autonomy of a separate nation, while at the same time, remaining our military allies relative to any invasion from outside America.

Dirk Aubrey Lokison

1983

Updated Commentary

In all of human history, there is no example of any multi-cultural society having survived. It has always led to the downfall of the society, because only those who create a great culture are capable of sustaining it. What works are indigenous peoples, enjoying race and culture preservation in absolute liberty as separate sovereign nations competing in a free world market. Only this, can lead to world peace and prosperity. We are tired of being victimized, and of explaining the facts to militant sleepwalkers. Revolution is at hand! Good people will, by any means necessary, make natural order prevail on this planet. Those who oppose us, dig your graves. Winter is coming.

Eric F. Magnuson
February 23, 2016
11:05 A.M.

"We often give our enemies the
means of our own destruction."

~ Aesop ~

Are Racial Outlanders Dangerous?

American Case History

This is the testimony of a man of European ancestry living in the United States. He will remain anonymous and withhold location information in order to preserve future options:

"When I was young, I had very liberal viewpoints, liked Jack Kennedy, and believed that all that government assistance would inspire the recipients to pull themselves up and become productive members of society, because that is how *I* would respond in their circumstances. This was very innocent of me, because I didn't understand the basic differences between people. Today I use the *N Word,* but in this context I prefer the term *Negro,* so as not to distract all the boot-licking Socialists from the content.

1962 Massachusetts
I'm walking along having a normal conversation with a
Malato student near campus dormitories, when he suddenly
jumps me. We wrestle, but he gets the better of me with a
choke hold. I say 'Okay, I give,' but that isn't enough. He
tightens his grip until I'm strangling. It's almost impossible to
talk, but I manage to tell him to let go, or I'll have to report
him to the school administration. He reminds me that nobody
is around, that he could kill me and nobody would
know, then he chokes me for another ten minutes. This is a
very bleak and frightening experience. Finally, he lets go.
and I tell him I have to head home. In the future I avoid him.

1964 Boston
My mother returns from shopping to her car. Before she can
lock the passenger door, a Negro jumps in and tries to rape
her. She manages to open the driver door and yells for help,
The Negro panics, jumps out, and runs away.

1968 San Francisco
A girlfriend of mine moves to San Francisco. Within two
weeks she is raped by a Negro.

1972 Boston
A friend of mine is returning home when a Negro pulls a
knife on him and demands his money. He complies, and
later talks to a girl who has been robbed this way fifteen
times in the past two years, always by Negroes.

1995 Northern California
I am diagnosed with a fatal tumor and referred to a
neurosurgeon. When I phone the office, the surgeon's
Mexican secretary can barely speak English. I express
dismay at this. She becomes sullen, angry, and
uncooperative. Finally she says she will put my file on his
desk. I call periodically about getting my appointment. Three
months pass, my condition becomes much worse. I will die
soon, and become so frightened that I seek administrative
remedy outside the surgical unit to bypass the secretary.

When I finally get my appointment, the surgeon apologizes.
It turns out that the secretary kept shifting my case folder to
the bottom of the pile on his desk. Although this is clearly
attempted murder, I don't pursue the matter at the time. To
do so would have reset the entire process and waiting
period. At last I get my surgery, but nearly die from
complications resulting from the delay. Later I look for the
secretary, and find out that she no longer works for the
surgeon. After a follow-up exam, I'm told that I will need a
second operation in 1997, so I decide to delay taking action.
There is no way to find out who she is without giving away
my intention.

1999 Northern California
In a traffic jam quick-stop, a white kid in a pickup truck
smashes into the back my car at about 60 mph, He is
listening to dirty mouth Negro rap music with a
subwoofer, and doesn't hear the noise of screeching tires
ahead of him. He doesn't see all the stopped cars, because
he is looking in his rearview mirror to see if the white family
behind him are properly impressed with his rebellious
demeanor. After an examination and a cat-scan at the
hospital, I'm told that I have a skull fracture and a herniated
lower lumbar vertebra. I am partially paralyzed in my right
leg to this day. In a good country, the installation of
subwoofers in vehicles would not be legal. They
are generally used by Negroes and Mexicans to make unjust
encroachment on white people.

2002 Nevada
I'm living in an apartment house with no other residence
options at the time. There is a very loud Mexican in the next
room. He never sleeps, and yells all night, every night. The
manager, also a Mexican, keeps telling me he will move the
loudmouth to another room the next time his rent comes
due, but it never happens. The typical excuse is that when
the yeller comes down to pay the rent, the girl on the desk
doesn't know the situation, and simply renews him for
another two months. This continues for six months. I am

getting only two hours sleep every night, because the Mexican doesn't stop until 4:00 A.M. Finally my resistance becomes so low I become deathly ill with pneumonia, This persists for six months, I become anemic, my muscles atrophy, and I am going to die. The hospital keeps me on an antibiotic intravenous for two weeks. When I get out, the loud Mexican is still there. He's half my age and twice my size, but I threaten to kill him, so he moves out.

2005 Nevada - Winter
I overhear a conversation between two Negroes at a bus stop, 'Yo, I got Brown Recluse. Carry in saltshaker. Put in Motherfucker's bed. That fix Motherfucker's ass.". How this works out I don't know. Naturally I'm curious, but feel that it might be impolite, or politically incorrect, to ask.

2005 Nevada - Spring
Am talking with a friend outdoors when a Negro, acting like an ostrich for some reason, comes up and grabs me. I shove him away. The Negro addresses two passing security officers, 'Did you see that? How he put his hands on me?' One of the officers replied, 'Yes, but I also saw what you did first.' The Negro looks disappointed and continues up the street as an ostrich.

One night, around 2:00 AM, in a public dormitory, on the lower bunk, I am awakened by my blanket being pulled off by a yelling Mexican on the upper bunk. I start to sit up. With a broad swipe, he claws me with his fingernails, drawing blood from my forehead about an inch above my right eye. He's raving incoherently, saying that I must leave the city immediately. I tell the security officer, who knows who the fellow is and says. "Oh, Jesus!" then goes over to calm him down. The Mexican now pretends to be asleep, so the security officer shines a flashlight in his face and awakens him to see if he's okay.

2005 Nevada - Summer
In the same dormitory, am awakened about 1:00 AM by the
conversation of security officers as they carry three
stationary men, one at a time, out of the dormitory. Next day
in a breakfast line, a friend tells me that he heard that three
dead white guys were removed from the dormitory, the
previous night. I never learn anything more about this, so
who knows what happened? I do remember, before I fell
asleep, seeing a Negro man prowling around in the dark like
he was studying possibilities.

One morning I'm waiting for a bus, and a mad-dog Negro
with no shirt, comes raging down the street shouting
and throwing stones at everyone and everything. I see him
and hide bend the bus kiosk. Too late, he sees me and
starts throwing at me. Then he crosses the street and opens
a big water main that starts flooding the area. In late
afternoon the water is still flooding as previously.

Another day, out front of a convenience store, a Negro asks
for money. When I refuse, he threatens that I will be hung by
his neighborhood friends. Then he walks a safe distance
away, and starts throwing stones at me. When the bus
arrives, he runs up and heaves a big cup full of ice inside,
hitting me, the driver, and two other passengers.

2005 Nevada - Autumn
I'm eating a nice chicken dinner at city social club, and get
talking with a friend at the table. He tells me that he became
an alcoholic because he could not get over the murder of his
fifteen year old daughter a few years earlier. He tried to warn
her, but a fast talking Negro boy managed to get her alone.
After he and a friend raped her, they cut her throat, and left
her to die behind a restaurant. A few years later, the father
got a call from his mother saying that two Negroes were
trying to break into her apartment. He arrived in time, and
shot them both in the head. In court he said, 'Two of these
people murdered my daughter. What was I supposed to do,
let them kill my *mother* too?' He was acquitted.

2008 Nevada
I need a follow-up MRI scan to check for recurrence of
the tumor. My doctor refers me to a Negro "neurologist" who
talks more like a gruff railroad worker. He says he will
schedule me for an MRI. Call to check at normal intervals
and always get the 'It takes time, Sir' routine from the
Mexican secretaries. Finally at five and a half months, I insist
that the secretary check the status of my scheduling, and am
told that nobody ever ordered the MRI.

2009 Nevada
I'm on the way to a film premiere on a double decker bus
when, from behind, a Negro pushes me into the stair well.
Somehow I keep my orientation so that I land on my feet, but
am badly lamed in both legs. Nobody sees it. I'm in too much
pain to beat up the Negro, besides this, it would be on the
security camera. I proceed, limping, to the premiere, and the
left leg still hurts me to this day.

For each of these events I have endured at least a hundred
arbitrary insults or threats, mostly from Negroes. As a race I
consider them the second foulest living things on Earth. Yes,
today I use the *N Word*. I say *No* to savages in America, and
I'll call them any goddamned thing I want. It's the prejudice of
experience. I've never had any problem with Asians or
Caucasians. I know that there are some nice black people,
but the benefit derived from them is massively outweighed
by the danger from the hordes of bad ones, and the relative
number is increasing. Tje honeymoon is over. Integration
has failed. Racial outlanders *are* dangerous.

In my lifetime I have watched my country slowly turned into a
quagmire of filth by the Globalist Shadow Government. What
we need is a fleet of ships sailing to Africa, not obese
welfare mammies mass-producing Negroes, like turds, at the
public expense. Let's do it now, because if an inspired leader
like Adolf Hitler comes to power in the United States, all
good European Americans are going to follow him to Hell
and back to purge our country of this subhuman pestilence."

C B P
December 21, 2015
9:57 A.M.

Indigenous Peoples Everywhere, Rise!

Liberty or Death!

Right to Bear Arms

In a free society, the individual has the legal right to own or carry abroad any weapon he chooses, except the intrinsically unsafe weapon. This is one that cannot possibly be used without injury to innocent bystanders. Even governments have no right to own such a weapon. The popular objection that an "assault" weapon is designed to kill people misses the main point. What else, other than hunting, would any liberty loving person want a weapon for? To kill flies? It is not flies who invade countries and private homes to rape, torture, and murder. It is people who do that.

The individual has the natural right not to be treated as a criminal before the fact of committing a crime. Owning a weapon is not evidence of intent. In a free society, it is up to the individual to decide what measures he will enact to insure the safety of his own person or home. These decisions must be made based upon his individual expectations about other people and the future of his country, and must not be usurped by "optimistic" pacifists who would slavishly thirst to lick the boots of an invading enemy rather than to ever resist anything. Observe that these cowardly collectivist life managers would gladly see their oppressive confiscatory laws enforced using deadly coercion if necessary by government bully-boys with guns. Learn well the names of the true enemies of liberty who reside within your own country.

Any individual advocating the confiscation or undue regulation of safe weapons in the hands of responsible citizens is a clear traitor to the country in which he lives. Such a person is guilty of treason, and will by liberty loving individuals, be dealt with as such immediately, using whatever means are available. Any government attempting to deny it's citizens the right to purchase and bear arms has been subverted, and will, by courageous spirited people, be thrown down immediately, using any degree of force necessary.

Defense of Borders

Indigenous populations commit racial and cultural suicide if they allow their country to be invaded. A sovereign nation, not run by traitors, will enforce its borders by any means necessary. The situation is like a contract. The country gives fair warning to potential invaders that if the borders are violated, deadly force will be used to stop the invasion.

Border policy should be announced via popular media, with ongoing warning given by signs. Once fair notice is given, there need be no consideration as to whether invaders are men, women, or children. Reprisal should be carried out as necessary using snipers, strafing from helicopters, and satellite lasers from space.

At this writing, the southern border of the United States has been under siege since 2014. If the United States is to survive as a nation, this invasion must be stopped. Every invader so far apprehended, should be deported, and if they come back, executed. It's perfectly just to resist invasion with deadly force, if people are made aware of the contractual terms in advance.

Islamic Conquest

Islamists have an average IQ of eighty. They believe that they are superior to everybody else on earth, and that it is their just destiny to rule, then destroy, everybody who differs from them in any way. These delusionary values are shared with their noticeably smarter 105 IQ Semitic kinsmen, the Jews.

Many in Europe and America have been saying lately,

"Almost every problem in the West, including our disabling cheek-turner religion, has come to us from the Hooknoses of the East."

Could it be time to fight back?

One standard diplomatic lie is that Mid-Eastern terrorists are considered extremists within their own countries. In truth, their actions are done with the full approval of the vast majority of Islamists. What we call terrorists are simply the military class within their own countries. The goal of Islam is world domination. The Quran is a blueprint for the conquest and subjugation of nations. When asked about this, Islamists excuse, "It is one of the lesser prophets." Their plan has four steps:

1. Infiltration
The advance guard comes in as "refugees" seeking humanitarian aid. They are, humble, soft spoken and friendly, at first, but always live parasitically on welfare.

2. Consolidation
During this period, the immigrants instruct the weak mined members of the host population in their religion and convert them. Mosques appear everywhere. Terrorist attacks begin, but the IMF subverted media doesn't report them.

3. Takeover
This is when the number of invaders becomes sufficient in various districts to elect their own officials to government. Now injustice in the courts favoring terrorists against the host population skyrockets.

4. Theocracy
Host population must convert to Islam, leave the country, or be killed.

Note that the Globalists are aiding and abetting the invaders via the European Union and the United Nations in entering Western Europe and the United States. Eastern European countries, however, are not admitting Islamists.

The Japanese have always been smart people. They welcome Buddhists, Christians, and Hindus, but not Islamists, because they know that Islam is not really a religion, but a method of conquest.

Sharia Law

Values passed down through generations eventually become ingrained genetic predispositions for behavior. Sharia Law proclaims that it is the right of Islamic men to rape women and children. By civilized western standards, the values of Islam are psychopathic and their sustenance for so long a time has made the practitioners into a race of constitutional psychopaths. Know a good one? Wake up! There are always a few exceptions to help underscore anything that is generally true.

Short Summary Sharia Law

Theft is punishable by amputation of the hands.
Denying any part of the Quran is punishable by death.

Criticizing Muhammad is punishable by death.

Criticizing Allah is punishable by death.

A Muslim who leaves Islam is punishable by death.

One who leads a Muslim out of Islam is punishable by death.

A non-Muslim man who marries a Muslim woman is punishable by death.

A woman or girl who has been raped cannot testify in court against her rapists.

Testimonies of four males is required to prove rape of a female.

A female who claims rape without producing four male witnesses is guilty of adultery.

A female found guilty of adultery is punishable by death.
 A male convicted of rape can have the conviction dismissed by marrying the victim.

If a child or a woman is taken captive, they become a slaves. A woman's previous marriage is immediately annulled.

A woman may be forced to marry a man whom she does not want.

A wife must have sex whenever her husband demands it.

Muslim men have sexual rights to any female not wearing the Hijab.

A woman can have one husband.

A man can have four wives.

A man can marry a female infant, and sexually consummate the marriage when she reaches nine years of age.

A girl's clitoris must be cut.

A man can beat his wife for disobedience.

A man can simply divorce his wife.

A wife needs the husband's consent to divorce.

A divorced wife loses custody of children when they reach six years of age.

A woman's court testimony in property cases, has half the veracity of a man's.

A female inherits half of what a male inherits.

A woman cannot speak alone to a man who is not her husband or relative.

Meat for meals must come from animals that have been sacrificed to Allah.

Muslims should lie to non-Muslims to advance Islam.

Liberty and Terrorism

Council of the Gods

May 3, 2002 11:02 AM

On C-Span 1 this morning there was a new statistic:

Forty eight percent of Americans polled believe that America is under the special protection of Jehovah in the Mid-Eastern War.

Awhile back on one of the cable news channels there was similar data about people throughout the Middle East believing that Allah is backing them militarily.

Since we have such perfect separation of church and state in America, it would be too much compromise to ask one of the Congressional prayer groups to intervene. We do, however, suggest that if the UN could somehow get Jehovah and Allah together for negotiations, the rest of us could simply stand aloof from the entire business. With the 2004 Olympic Games to be held in Athens, perhaps a summit could be arranged on Mount Olympus.

Objective View of Political Terrorism

November 23, 2002

Comments we have received trigger the following response. In the longer view of history the following things are true:

1. Political terrorists in general are far more concerned about impacting public events and history than the average person.

2. Political terrorists are usually revolutionaries who also believe that their agenda for long term social change is more important than individual human lives. This latter trait is often shared by functionaries of the governments they oppose.

3. Those who disagree with specific terrorist goals often avoid dealing with the political issues by trying to shift attention away using phony psychological "explanations." This will often involve highlighting any lack of standard affiliations or personal involvements in the life of the terrorist which might have otherwise consumed personal energies: "He was a loner who didn't belong to any clubs on campus." "He was angry at society because he wasn't getting enough nookie."

4. The viewpoint of political terrorists and most "lunatic fringe" elements can be useful as part of the advance warning system about bad directions in government policy. In this context the more "sensitive" terrorist reactions may be likened to the quicker response of those small birds taken underground in cages to test the breathability of air in mines.

June 21, 2017 9:32 A.M.

War and terrorism today are a very difficult study. Just when you think you understand an event, new information surfaces showing that it was actually a false flag, usually involving Globalist traitors in your own government working with foreign operatives. The purpose of endless war is to generate "refugees" aided by EU and the UN, to invade and destroy indigenous race and culture, so that people lacking identity will except globalization.

Terrorism is supported by deep state funding, open borders, and, police stand-downs. The purpose is to make our daily lives so dangerous that we will gladly surrender our guns and liberty just to feel safe. Good people need to become proactive about building a better future. We will be rid of these problems only when the Globalists and their invading outlanders have been permanently defeated.

Challenge of Street Terrorism

Within the borders of any country, street terrorists are usually just psychopathic enemies of society in general, rarely people with any reasoned political motivation. Their numbers are increasing everywhere. In any country where criminals are protected by corrupt socialist governments, this army of darkness can only be dealt with on an individual basis. It's always best to keep a low profile by simply humoring subverted cowards who try to tell you that the victim is just as bad as the criminal if he retaliates.

You have the natural right to defend your life and property. and to rid your country of evil people. Every person willing to fight back should carry a pistol, sword cane, or stun gun. If attacked or threatened, he should kill all the assailants .
There will be that many less of them in the world, and he will never have to fight them a second time. He should leave the vicinity immediately, keep his own council, and tell absolutely nobody what happened. The weak character trait of compulsive intimacy is no substitute for the personal integrity gained through unimpeded righteous action.

Specifically: The Knockout Game

November 30, 2013 9:00 AM
This morning a neighbor told me about a new phenomenon known as the "knockout game" now happening in America. Last week he was nearly assaulted by three young Mexicans, but used his cane in self-defense. He said the TV news claims that three victims have been killed already. I looked it up online. The Internet news says that the problem is beginning to appear nationwide in the USA. Remember the immortal wisdom of Bernard Goetz,
"Speed is everything."

Human Trafficking: A Few Facts

Victims:

Children and adults for sex, labor, and service

Statistics:

Human trafficking is a $150 billion industry worldwide, the third largest international crime industry after illegal drugs and arms trafficking.

80% is sexual exploitation

19% is labor exploitation

25% are children

75% are women and girls

The International Labor Organization claims that there are 40.3 million living victims of human trafficking worldwide.

The U.S. State Department says that, 600,000 to 800,000 people are trafficked across international borders every year.

Between 14,500 and 17,500 people are trafficked into the U.S. each year.

The International Labor Organization estimates that women and girls represent the largest share of forced labor with 11.4 million trafficked (55%) compared to 9.5 million (45%) men.

The U.S. Department of Labor identifies 148 different products from 75 countries made by forced labor.

In 2017, one out of seven runaways reported to the National Center for Missing and Exploited Children were child sex trafficking victims.

Of these, 88% were in the care of social services or foster care when they ran away.

Eighty percent of children sold into sexual slavery are under 24, some as young as six.

The average age for the sex trade in the U.S. is 12 to 14 years old. Many of the runaway girls were sexually abused as children.

At this writing, there is one internet pedophile ring in the U.S. with 70,000 members.

Five noteworthy points about Globalist pedophile trafficking:

- the tens of thousands of people involved

- the high rank and tremendous wealth of many of the participants

- the activities, especially torture, mutilation, blood drinking, and gourmet cannibalism

- the involvement of those we should be able to trust, like CIA, Vatican, United Nations

- the automatic protection of participants by subverted government officials and media

Most human trafficking in the United States occurs in New York, California, and Florida.

California has three of the FBI's highest child sex trafficking cities in the nation: Los Angeles, San Francisco, and San Diego.

The National Human Trafficking Hotline receives more calls from Texas than any other state, 15% from the Dallas-Fort Worth area.

Trafficking plays a major role in spread of HIV.

30,000 victims of sex trafficking die each year from abuse, disease, torture, and neglect.

Sudanese phrase: "use a slave to catch slaves." Traffickers send "broken-in girls" to recruit younger girls into the sex trade.

Sex traffickers often train girls themselves, first raping, then teaching them sex acts.

71% of trafficked children become suicidal.

UNICEF estimates that 300,000 children younger than 18 are currently trafficked to serve in armed conflicts worldwide. Often they serve as suicide bombers.

Traffickers target victims on the telephone, the Internet, through friends, at the mall, and through after-school programs.

Traffickers often work with corrupt government officials to obtain travel documents and seize passports.

Traffickers are increasingly taking pregnant women for the newborns. Babies are sold on the black market. The profit is divided between traffickers, doctors, lawyers, border officials.

People are trafficked for organ harvesting.

Increasing numbers of trafficked children are being terrorized, drained of adrenalized blood, then prepared and eaten like piglets or turkeys.

Per capita, there are more human slaves in the world today than ever before in history.

Due to globalization, every continent of the world has been involved in human trafficking.

Slaves are cheaper than they have ever been in history. The population explosion has resulted in a huge supply of potential workers. Globalization has created a mindset and environment where people are vulnerable and easily enslaved.

Worldwide, average cost of a slave is $90.

Globalism: Logical Fallacies

It is important to study logic because most logical fallacies seem more or less reasonable, even though they are not. Sometimes there is innocent intent with error, but more often, there is a deliberate attempt to misdirect. Among the controlled media subverted to Globalism, there are a great many today who have studied hard upon the "engineering of consent."

This presentation uses examples of standard Globalist arguments as they are countered by those of Libertarian Nationalism. Sometimes examples are left to the reader. Fallacies are divided into four standard categories. Some fit into more than one category and, of course, many arguments involve more than one fallacy.

August 9, 2017
9:46 A/M.

Fallacies of Relevance
Arguments to Cases Not Relevant

Ad Baculum
Appeal to Force
Might Makes Right

Example:
New World Order goals are correct because men of great
power support them

Genetic Fallacy:
Suggests that the origin of something necessarily
determines its essence and character

Example:
"He comes from a background of privation, so he will
naturally support our Socialist agenda."

Ad Hominem
Addresses opponent instead of his argument

First type:

Abusive
Name Calling
Often involves phony psychologizing

Examples:
You are called a *racist* if you if you work to preserve all races
and cultures.

You are called a *homophobe* if you do not support teaching
children in the public schools that same-gender sex
perversion is really just an equal alternative lifestyle.

You are called an *Islamophobe* if you do not support the
slow takeover of your country by Islam, as in Europe today.

Second type:

Circumstantial
Categorizing
Opponent should accept an argument because of his circumstances or category

Example:
"You are a Democrat, so you must support all Democratic Party policies."

Guilt by Association
Water Seeks its Own Level
Birds of a Feather Flock Together
One's character is judged totally by the company he keeps

Example:
"He has meetings so often with the Russians, so he must be on their payroll."

Poisoning the Well
Mud Slinging
Presenting negative, especially false, information about a person before they speak so as to discredit their argument

Example:
Most of what Globalists say about Nationalists

Gaslighting
Attempt to invalidate a person's experiences by twisting facts, memories, events, and evidence in order to disorient a vulnerable opponent and make them doubt their own judgement

Example:
Globalist media spokesmen regularly make claims and then, when challenged, deny ever having made them

Ad Populum
Attempts to validate an argument by citing a plurality or majority consensus

Three subcategories:

Bandwagon
"Everybody supports it."

Example:
It is an obligation of government to provide ongoing livelihood for the "disenfranchised" because immigrant third world savages, seeking sustenance, and their subverted accomplices, vastly outnumber good people at the voting booths

Patriot
Flag waving at the opponent to imply that he is not loyal to his country

Snob
"All the best people support it."

Example:
"Many of the Globalists are bluebloods."

Appeal to Tradition
Premise is true because people have always believed it

Example:
"Two inescapable verities, death and taxes."

A Priori Argument
Dogmatism
Starts with as established belief, then searches for any reasonable-sounding argument to defend the argument based upon it.

Example:
False assumption that if there are economic differences
between two racial groups at any fixed point in time that
there must be foul play involved. Therefore government must
implement "social justice" by victimizing the more successful
group. Ignores history.

The *More Righteous for Not Questioning* version of A Priori
is liked by religious fanatics.

Example:
With enflamed piety,
"Don't speak to me of reason.
Don't confuse me with facts.
Don't confound me with logic.
Don't burden me with truth.
The anointed one is my redeemer,
And I will not disobey!"

Appeal to Improper Authority
One claims that his argument is right because someone
famous or powerful supports it

Example:
Sound economic policies must be wrong because famous,
uneducated, Hollywood twits make impassioned, but
treasonous, threats against those who support them.

Ad Misericordiam
Appeal to emotion or pity
Often ignores the long term

Example:
"By 1920, Ludwig Von Misses had proved everything that
Karl Marx ever postulated."
"But ... poor people are suffering."

Adverse Consequences
Conclusion must be false because the consequences of it
being true are just too terrible to contemplate

Example:
"My heart tells me that that no major religion could ever
endorse or condone rape."
Guess what? Islam does. Wake up!

Personal Incredulity
Argument must be false because you don't understand its
technicalities

Example:
"We can't eliminate the personal income tax. How will we
pay for government?"

Grasping at Straws
Desperate citing of unrelated irrelevancies

Example:
"Are you for or against Socialism?"
"I believe we should all love each other, nobody understands
another person's feelings, you should think about being in
the other person's shoes, what about poverty, what happens
if we have to eat pigeons and rats?"

Snow Job
Smoke Screen
Blizzard or cloud of distraction used deliberately to cover up
the main issues
Example:
Ongoing rhetoric of Globalist media

Anecdotal
Uses a personal experience or an isolated example instead
of a sound argument

Example:
"Their economic proposals remind me of the time my cousin Lucy got locked inside the neighbors' outhouse in a snowstorm. The neighbors were away, and she was missing in there for three days. When the police finally found her … well, you can just imagine …"

Pedantry
Last Refuge of Little Minds
Jumping on a minor spelling or pronunciation problem, grammatical error, or typo to distract from the substance of the argument.

Example:
In an Email letter:
"It's wrong that American women are being told they must wear berkas."

Email reply:
"I'm sorry, but the term is *burkas*."

Component Fallacies
Errors in Syllogistic Reasoning

Begging the Question
Premise and conclusion say the same thing
Often ignores slow changes over time

Example:
"Recreational drugs don't hurt us, because we are back to normal the next morning."

Circular Reasoning
Phrasing premise and conclusion in different words that mean the same thing

Example:
"Absolute individual liberty will present a danger to society, because society cannot be safe if people are truly free."

Glib Generalization
Jumping to Conclusions
Cannot See the Forest for the Trees
One uses too small a sample to support a sweeping generalization. This often involves reasoning backwards inductively from an exceptional particular instance to a false general premise

Example:
Some high IQ members of a genetically inferior group are able to succeed, so they all can.
Therefore evolved societies should be ruined to give special advantage to Stone Age people.

False Cause
References a cause-effect relationship that does not exist

Two common types:

Non Causa Pro Causa
Mistaking a false cause for a real cause

Example:
"Free thinking led to all this drug use."
In truth, Prohibition created a huge black market profit
potential that led to a program of aggressive marketing we
call *pushing*.

Post Hoc, Ergo Propter Hoc
After this, therefore because of this
Assumes that correlation equals causation.
If one circumstance occurs in proximity to another, then it
must be the cause of it.

Example:
"The excess love of whiskey in the 1920s caused the terrible
gang wars of that period."
In real life, it was the inability of bootleggers to arbitrate
disputes in the courts that caused the gang wars. Prohibition
was the cause. Make court actions illegal in real estate
disputes, and watch the murder rate go sky high.

Ignorantio Elenchi
Irrelevant Conclusion
Argument used to establish a particular conclusion by
redirecting it back as though evidenced by a more general
related premise which may, or may not, be true.

Example:
A proposal is under consideration for increase in immigration
by racially incompatible people.
"It is desirable for society to have a diverse racial and ethnic
population."
To guilt ridden self-haters, this seems self-evident. They all
agree. Later...
"My proposal is this...like I said at the beginning ... it is
desirable to have a diverse ... therefore I move that we ..."

The entire premise is false. Historically there has never been even one multi-racial society that did not self-destruct because of the forced unnatural mixing.

A subcategory of Ignorantio Elenchi is

The Red Herring
Changing the subject to avoid answering

Example:
"Marxism doesn't work."
"All people are entitled to personal dignity."
Another form of the Red Herring is

Tu Quoque
"And you too!"
An argument must be false because the person presenting it doesn't follow it himself.

Example:
"We need to take back our streets."
"We do?? I never see *you* out at night."

Yet another Red Herring is the

Straw Man Argument
Takes one of an opponent's weaker, less central, arguments, refutes it, then acts as though it was the crux of the issue. This is usually done using exceptional particulars.

Example:
"All those poor people who accidentally shoot themselves at home would still be alive if guns were banned."
Ignores the vastly greater number who have been murdered in no-gun zones because they had no way to defend themselves. In 2016, 400 people in Chicago alone.

Non Sequitur
Argument does not follow from the previous.

Usually ignores many other considerations

Example
"Use of energy is too high. We must have a carbon tax."
Energy use is too high because there are nearly 8 billion
people on Earth when there should be 320 million.

Another specific type of Non Sequitur is the

Slippery Slope Fallacy
Argues that, once a step is taken, more steps of negative
consequence will inevitably follow

Example:
"If you encourage liberty and individuality, it will most
certainly lead to cultural divisiveness."
Strong cultures are good, bring it on!

False Dichotomy
Harbors the premise that there are only two possible
solutions, therefore disproving one automatically validates
the other. Ignores other alternatives

Example:
In cases of snuff porn video makers, "Rehabilitation therapy
with parole is the best solution, because long, fixed periods
of incarceration don't work."
Ignores the fact that death is the only effective way of ridding
society of the threat posed by the proven irredeemable evil
inherent in constitutional psychopathy.

False Analogy
Phony comparison to prove a point rather than arguing
deductively and inductively

Example:
"Freedom is like pepper. A little tastes good, but too much
gives you indigestion."

Undistributed Middle Term
The minor and major premise of a syllogism might or might
not overlap. The falseness is usually obvious or even funny,
but not always.

Example:
"Libertarians engage in free thought.
Crooks engage in free thought.
Therefore Libertarians are crooks."

Contradictory Premises
Logical Paradox
Premise contradicts another earlier premise

Example:
"We need to construct Holocaust study programs so that it
can never happen again."
Sorry, but there is no hard evidence that it ever happened in
the first place.
See essay, *World War II and Causes*

Special Pleading
Suggests a universal principle, then insists that it does not
apply to the issue at hand

Example:
"Monogamous relationships are the norm because they give
people what they truly need. Prostitution must therefore
remain illegal."
Ignores the fact that prostitution also gives many other
people what *they* truly need without detriment to anyone.
Globalists don't want free enterprise prostitutes to compete
with their human trafficking operations.

Ad Nauseum
Sickening Repetition
Where there's Smoke, there's Fire

Repeating a statement too often in the hopes that the listener will begin to accept it as truth, instead of providing evidence.

Example:
Phony Russian narrative touted by subverted Globalist media. Totally disproved, but reintroduced every two weeks

False Claims
Argument based upon false claims, but is logically coherent

Example:
"How could they have good intentions, when they murdered six million innocent people?"

Retrospective Determinism
Argues that because something happened, it was inevitable.
Example:
"Taking back Danzig was bound to lead to war sooner or later."

Texas Sharpshooter
Where there is smoke, there is fire
Occurs when one sees an apparent pattern of data and applies to their argument

Example:
"He has so many conversations with the Russian Prime Minister, he must be a spy."

Missing the Point
The premise supports a conclusion different from the one drawn

Example:
"Fuel prices are much too high, so speed limits will have to be lowered."

Fuel prices are too high for many reasons unrelated to speed, besides, slower speeds do not reduce fuel consumption.

Spotlight Fallacy
Exploits the false assumption that events which receive the most publicity are also the most common

Example:
This trick is used by subverted Globalist media bosses to destroy race and culture by instilling unwarranted guilt and self-hatred in host populations: In America, white on nonwhite crime is made front page news over and over, enflamed by phony editorials and bills to Congress about white racism. Nonwhite on white crime is buried on page four with no mention of race. This has been done by Jewish media bosses in America since 1945. Ride the city bus every day to see the result.

Misnomer Fallacy
Defending an absurdity by calling it something it is not. Often ignores the longer term

Example:
The breed-up-quick crowd refer to race mixing as *diversity*. In actuality it is just the opposite, because over time it would ultimately obliterate all individual races, resulting in *grey slavery*. Real diversity is indigenous populations in separate sovereign nations competing in a free world market, with travelers enjoying potent undiluted cultures.

Stereotype
A stereotype is the random generalization that an individual member of an identifiable group, for better or for worse, probably possesses a particular characteristic which is alleged to, but may or may not, be especially common among members of the group. Stereotypes are often based upon race, nationality, sex, and age, but only become harmful when used to make judgements of consequence

about a person, without any substantive knowledge of the person as an individual.

Example:
 "Watch out, or them corn-servatives will call you a pre-vert and summon the poe-lice."

False Grouping Stereotype
The notion that ideas must me embraced as package deals

Example:
If someone supports gun ownership, they must, of course, oppose a woman's right to choose about abortion.

Category Error
Attributing a property to something that could not possibly have that property

Incomplete Comparison
Two things are compared that are not related, in order to make something more appealing than it really is

Quoting Out of Context
When an original phrase is distorted by quoting it out of context

Etymological Fallacy
Posits that a term's original meaning applies to its colloquial and modern understanding in current circumstances

Gambler's Fallacy
Belief that likelihood of a specific event can be effected by unrelated events, or that something has happened so often in the past that it is less likely that it will happen in the future.

Inflation of Conflict
Belief that instances where so many scholars have differing opinions, that this in itself calls the credibility of the entire field into question. Therefore no action should be taken.

These last four were used at Nuremberg.
Read the transcripts for yourself.

Kettle Logic
Use of several inconsistent arguments to defend a position

Shotgun Argumentation
Too many arguments for the opponent to answer them all

Proof by Verbosity
Argument too complicated and verbose for opponent to
address all the particulars

Intimidation
Person making argument is so well-respected that everyone
takes his claims as truth

Fallacies 0f Ambiguity
Change of Meanings in Discussion
Render Arguments Fallacious

Equivocation
Making equivalent things that are not

Example:
Referring to the *country*, the *people,* and the *government* as
though they were one thing. *Country* is a geographically
defined area within which exists the potential for absolute
individual liberty. *Government* is that group of subverted
collectivist traitors in the service of international finance who
prevent this liberty from occurring. The *people* are that
majority of brainwashed, deluded individuals who aid and
abet government in doing this.

Reification
Misplaced concreteness

Example:
"We will stop Libertarian truth with censorship."

Composition
Reasoning from of the parts of the whole to the whole itself

Example:
"Libertarianism is a sham."
"Why?"
"It won't pay for sex change."
Division
Argues that what is true of the whole must be true of
individual parts

Amphiboly
Grammatical construction causes ambiguity
Hedging

Use of a double meaning or an unclear description applied to mislead or misrepresent the truth, then changing the meaning of the terms later. This is often done by politicians.

Fallacies of Omission
Absence of Necessary Information

Stacking the Deck
Ignores examples that disprove the point

Example:
"Libertarians are always libertines."

No True Scotsman Fallacy
Stacking the deck by defining terms narrowly to exclude
relevant examples

Example:
"Bolshevists were evil. They murdered sixty-six million
people during their revolution."
"Yes, but their revolution was for the future of *Russia*. Forty
six million of the casualties were Ukrainians and Poles."

Ad Ignorantium
Appeal to Ignorance

Example:
We should not establish a truly Libertarian society because
there has never been one in the past, so we cannot know
what bad things might come of it.

Ad Speculum
Hypothesis contrary to fact

Example:
 "In America, whites owe blacks bigtime."

In the USA, virtually all black people are descended from
those who were brought to America as slaves. Most white
people in America, however, are not descended from
southern plantation owners, and have inherited no culpability
in any of this. The presence of black people in America is,

for most white people, simply an unjust cultural and gene pool encroachment.

Another related lie is that all free people were unjustly enriched by the institution of slavery. In truth, the only people who gained from slavery were the plantation owners. Everybody else was hurt because of what it did to the price of commodities and the labor market. The slavery lies are used to promote so called "social justice" via mandatory wealth redistribution.

Complex Question
Loaded Question
Implies that another unproven statement is true without evidence or discussion

Example:
"How many deaths from overdose will be acceptable to you Libertarians, if we repeal Prohibition relative to heroin?" Ignores the fact that before Provision there was no epidemic in drug use, because there was no black market profit potential to sell it.

Argument from the Negative
Approach-Avoidance Conflict
Running to Extremes
One position is untenable, so the opposite must be true

Example:
Right wing extremist parent produces
left wing extremist child, who produces right wing extremist child, who produces left wing extremist child … ad infinitum.

Doublethink
Collectivist government favorite for adding insult to injury by naming harmful policies the exact opposite of what they are. The truth is totally omitted.

Formal Examples:
Monetary Control Act
Bank Secrecy Act
Homeland Security Act
Patriot Act

Casual Examples:
Friendly Fire
Collateral Damage
Enhanced Interrogation

Survival in North America

Survival Strategies:

1. Wealth

Facts:

The Forces of Darkness reign everywhere. Globalism is the enemy.

It is Evil to pay taxes to this enemy whenever this can be avoided legally.

Strategy:

Disdain material things completely. Sell everything that you can live without.

Achieve total liquidity. Enable instant mobility. Learn the science of invisibility.

2. Health

Facts:

Most in health care providers today have immense situational power. Evil exemplars, via willful negligence, can and sometimes do, select for extermination whomever they please.

Strategy:

Avoid hostile territory or large congregations of un-Libertarian elements.

Attain hand to hand martial prowess and appropriate weapon skills.

Preserve health with proper food, supplements, fluids, deep breathing, exercise, right-thinking, meditation, and Yoga.

3. Pleasure

Facts:

Most sought-after pleasures are costly, frivolous, and produce dependency.

Keeping a good outlook makes nearly everything pleasurable without disadvantage.

Strategy:

Travel to enjoy what's left before it's gone. Look carefully. Remember what you see. Take photos. Maybe we can restore some of it later.

4. Intellect

Facts:

It's more useful to accumulate memory based on fact than on speculation or fiction.

Ancient mythology is real in an archetypal sense, even though it is frequently not actual.

The aware volitional use of make-believe, as in goal oriented visualization augmented by archetypal imagery, is a very useful tool but should never become an end in itself.
Strategy:

Read voraciously. Learn much. Never display knowledge unnecessarily.

Seek information from all viewpoints especially "forbidden" sources. Keep opinions to yourself.

Study all things which truly interest. Allow interests to change radically and quickly.

Develop a very broad and balanced learning program. Practice many arts.

Be careful to focus on utility and avoid spreading oneself too thinly.

Bone up on areas previously neglected as you discover what these are.

Read Revisionist History. Enjoy accurate historical novels.

5. Spirit

Facts:

For every element in any religious tradition there is usually a parallel element in all other traditions. Differences generally involve only emphasis. Variations will occur even among individuals within any one tradition. A deep understanding of one's own ancient spiritual heritage is archetypally more relevant and closer to the bone than inappropriate involvement with "outland" traditions.

Reincarnation seems to be the best explanation of how life works in the long term. Cases abound.

Strategy:

Study appropriate early religious heritage and mythology.

Plan your next incarnation as a hypothetical upgrade for personal insight. Base plan upon how you would live your past life if you had it to do over again, but with current technology. Update this periodically for personal growth.

Help those terminally ill towards peace and happy anticipation of future life.

Practice true chivalry in its modern form. Always be polite and just.

Never cause any unnecessary pain or suffering to any living creature. This should apply even to the vilest of human enemies. Kill only to preserve life and liberty, but do this quickly and cleanly.

Be kind to all people and animals. Show affection to parents, children, dogs, and kitties.

6. Activism

Facts:

The individual is born with the right to absolute individual liberty. With this comes the logical obligation of reciprocity towards others. If the individual lives in an unfree society, he has the right to gain total individual liberty any way that he can. People who don't want to be free are cowards. Those who do not want others to be free are morally inferior and expendable, the mortal enemies of all decent people.

One world government will spell the end of liberty on Earth. It will institute an absolute monopoly for a small group of greedy internationalists. The one clear enemy of all people on Earth are those striving towards the New World Order. These individuals must be defeated at any cost. Separate sovereign nations competing in a free world market is better than the tedious cookie-cutter sameness portended by advancing global monoculture.

The preference to live and manifest among one's own kind is a trait, which during man's evolutionary development, became genetically ingrained as a natural instinct because it had survival value during periods of fierce tribal competition for food and shelter. People are naturally more aesthetically content, and feel far more at ease, among members their own people. This is a perfectly normal trait and cannot correctly be perceived as anything other than that. It is proper to respect the right of all individuals who justly strive to preserve their own race from destruction.

Freedom of religion best helps people to find their natural level of manifestation. This does not mean that we need condone those who ruthlessly seek dominion over everyone around them. Tolerance among separate unique religious traditions is vastly superior to the bland faceless beehive spirituality of worldwide universalism.

People who are obsessed with trying to reconcile modern experience with scriptures written thousands of years ago are being false to their own heritage and to the present day world. Slavish dogmatism renders the individual an ineffective participant in modern society. No one need look to another culture for their spirituality, nor aid and abet the missionaries of monoculture. Nobody should adhere to any tradition which has clearly failed. Religions based upon false values and unnatural principles are not worth following. The vile dispiriting nihilism of wandering internationalists is a poor substitute for the spiritual integrity of being rooted in one's own ancestral tradition. There are many fine natural religions being reborn. These represent diverse ethnicity. One must seek, however. They will not come to you.

Spiritual dualism involves absolute knowledge that good and evil are coequal, eternal, and cosmic in manifestation. Spiritual monism is the popular belief that either good or evil is the predominant moral force on Earth. This involves imaginative wishfulness about the supposed destiny of one to eventually triumph over the other. In this mode of error, one force is thought of as being a mere pathological deviation which can somehow be cured. Ironically, such ongoing cures institutionalized by collective human action have been responsible for most of the real evil and suffering faced by human societies throughout the ages. The idea that "good" is the prevailing force in the universe and will someday obliterate "evil," and that there is not supposed to be any suffering in the world, is the fantasy of weaklings, and usually leads to the kind of fanaticism exploited by power hungry leaders to the great detriment of all.

Absolute separation of church and state is impossible because the spirituality of the people determines the form of government they will choose or condone. The ultimate test of workability for a major system of religious belief is the effect that it has on society over the long term. A viable spirituality intended to exert major influence will not only attract widespread adherence but will also have a positive effect upon society. Monistic spirituality attracts many people but does so only because it appeals to human weakness by promising supernatural justice to apathetic sluggards. It is passive and limp-wristed. It contributes to all that is devolutionary. Wherever we find the institutionalized cowardice of scarecrow religion, we also find Socialism or some other unworkable form of collectivist government. The economic system of a country will never exceed the soul wisdom of the people residing therein. We can't expect an inferior prevailing spirituality to result in a superior way of running society. If the people are no good, the government will be even worse.

The religions based upon spiritual monism are acquiescent slave traditions. The practitioners are morally weak, simple-minded, cowardly, or insane. Most are all of these things. Their actions are rarely at one with their words. Individually they are impotent, but in larger numbers, each fueling the sickness of the others, they will become as torturous and murderous as their combined strength and self-serving rationalizations allow them to be.

The monistic majority is responsible for allowing the Socialism which now besieges us all. Certain elements within monism sponsored and now exploit this Socialism.

Unrestricted influx will destroy whatever is achieved anywhere. No country should allow vast throngs of fools who have out-bred their ability to feed themselves at home to come flooding in only to do the same thing in their new country as well.

The means to these ends should be contemplated dispassionately. Creative energy must be diligently applied to their implementation.

Strategy:

Avoid unproductive entanglement by restricting relationships to an absolute minimum.

Do not mix unnecessarily with un-Libertarian elements.

Help to promote worldwide Libertarian Nationalist Revolution to the utmost.

Educate others anonymously. Simply put superior knowledge within their grasp.

Write the best that you know. Reach those in places of power and learning.

The ideal attitude if one survives, even in a world decimated, is to continue in chivalrous Libertarian manifestation for as long as possible.

Ritual für den Tod

"Rise those who despise the weak
Spare none and ride proudly
on the winds of death"
~ Immortal ~

The following is a spur for the preservation of the Nordic Race, a declaration of war against sub-humanity everywhere and against racial outlanders who invade Nordic territories. Ritually it can be inserted as the "Statement of Purpose" within any format used by Nordic kindreds or communities.

Portent of Victory

"We shall ride triumphantly
through the streets in bright armor,
upon white horses, the corpses of these
impotent weakling slaves of darkness
lining the walkways at each side,
their blood running out and
filling the gutters at our feet!

"Then shall begin their conversion
into ash for our fields,
and the recasting by fire
of their holy chalices and idols,
of gold under Sun,
of silver under Moon,
from icons of shame and meekness
into gleaming images of Truth.

"And we shall fashion their holy places
into strongholds of voluptuousness,
their skulls will adorn the rafters
and gaze down upon us
as we enjoy our naked women
upon their holy altars."

Notes:

1. Nordic Race: of European ancestry, Caucasian, White.

2, "Portent of Victory" written long ago by Elof II.

New World Order

Short History

In 1773, Meier Amschel Rothschild met in Frankfurt, Germany with twelve of his most influential friends. He convinced them that by pooling their resources, they could rule the world. Rothschild soon found a man of incredible intelligence and ingenuity to head their organization, one Adam Weishaupt, a professor of Canon law. and Jesuit priest.

At the request of Rothschild and his friends, Weishaupt abandoned the Catholic Church, and created the secret Order of the Illuminati, on May 1, 1776. The objectives were, through currency manipulation via central bank control, and the cooperation of subverted politicians, to establish what they called a New World Order, which will seek:

Abolition of all ordered governments
Abolition of private property
Abolition of inheritance
Abolition of patriotism
Abolition of family
Abolition of religion
Creation of world government

Concern about the unelected power of international bankers arose as Congress prepared to extend a twenty-year charter with the Bank of the United States, a private central bank formed in 1816. Andrew Jackson vigorously opposed efforts to strengthen the grasp of any central bank over the U.S. He called private central bankers a "den of vipers" and in 1832 vetoed a bill to renew the charter.

Thomas Jefferson warned,

"If the American people ever allow private banks to control the issue of their currency, first by inflation and then by deflation, the banks and corporations that will grow up around them will deprive the people of all property until their children wake up homeless on the continent their fathers conquered."

The New World Order's power is nearly total today, with presidents, senators, congressmen, and mainstream media bosses among the subverted. The opposition to banker monopoly has shifted from those who govern to those who are governed, the people directly affected by the banker's totalitarian agenda.

Alexander Solzhenitsyn, in a speech at an AFL-CIO meeting, July 1975, spoke of a turning point where our hierarchy of values may waiver or collapse:

"The political crisis of today's world and the oncoming spiritual crisis, are occurring at the same time. It is our generation that will have to confront them."

Globalism and the Federal Reserve

The Federal Reserve Bank is the central bank of the United States. Out of thin air, by *fiat*, it creates paper currency and regulates the US money supply. Despite the misleading name, it is not part of the federal government. It is a private corporation owned by a cartel of international banking firms. The list of creditor-shareholders appears below.

The argument used by the bankers has always been that they can do a better job of managing things, so the government should borrow currency the bankers create by fiat, rather than create it on their own.

George Washington and other presidents kept the international bankers from taking over the issuing of currency for one hundred and twenty-four years. During this time there was a period of ninety years with total monetary stability, no rise in consumer prices at all. The only taxes were on real estate, tobacco, and liquor, and this was during the time of greatest immigration and road building in all of human history.

It wasn't until 1913 that the increasing number of corrupt politicians and media bosses made a banker takeover possible. Both the Federal Reserve Act and the Internal Revenue Act were debated in Congress, but many say that neither was properly ratified, and for that reason are both unlawful. This, of course, is a moot point, since both are unnecessary, destructive, and based on deception. The banker friendly controlled media has been ever vigilant in making the American people believe that both are not only lawful, but worthwhile. The entire swindle hinges only upon mass public ignorance about the facts presented here.

To *nationalize* the Federal Reserve Bank is simply to return the power to issue and regulate currency to the people through their government, which will no longer have to borrow or pay back the money. The unnecessary federal income tax pays only the interest on the unnecessary national debt which is now at nearly twenty trillion dollars.

Most other nations have a central bank equivalent in function to the US Federal Reserve. The globalist regulating agency for the entire worldwide banking cartel is called the International Monetary Fund. To get things back in balance, countries everywhere need to nationalize their central banks, repudiate their national debts, and demand reparation for the amount already swindled by the globalist creditors, as a civil alternative to being put on trial for engineering every war and ruined economy over the past two hundred years, or being the beneficiary heirs thereto, all of which is easily provable from existing historical records. This should be followed by a return to currencies backed by durable commodity of intrinsic value, like gold or a mixed store of precious metals, the value of which is determined in world markets.

US Federal Reeve Bank Shareholders:
Rothschild of London, Berlin
Lazard Brothers Banks of Paris
Israel Moses Seif Banks of Italy
Warburg Amsterdam. Hamburg
Lehman Brothers of New York
Kuhn, Loeb Bank of New York
Goldman, Sachs of New York
Levi P. Morton of New York
Hanover Trust of New York

Thomas Jefferson
3rd President of the
United States

"I believe that banking institutions are more dangerous to our liberties than standing armies. If the American people ever allow private banks to control the issue of their currency, first by inflation, then by deflation, the banks and corporations that will grow up around [these banks] will deprive the people of all property until their childern wake-up homeless on the continent their fathers conquered. The issuing power [of currency] should be taken from the banks and restored to the people, to whom it properly belongs."

World War II and Causes

Relatively Common Knowledge
Bankers and Subverted Politicians
"Lending Requires Spending"

Hebrew goals in early fiction unite them as a tribe.
Isaiah 60, 61 Covenant promise of Jehovah to the Israelites:
"Therefore, thy gates shall be open...that men may bring
unto thee the wealth of the Gentiles...For the nation and
kingdom that will not serve thee shall perish...Thou shalt also
suck the milk of the Gentiles...Ye shall eat the riches of the
Gentiles, and in their glory shall ye boast yourselves."

1917 Russian Revolution
Jewish Communists murder and confiscate the property of
twenty million Christians.

March 1919 First Communist Party Comintern Congress
Of the three hundred ninety three delegates, all but
seventeen are Jews.

June 1919 Treaty of Versailles
There is no evidence that Germany started World War I, but
with the help of baker accomplice, Colonel Edward Mandell
House, Germany is blamed for the war, forced to

demilitarize, give up large territories, and pay huge reparations, so the bankers can lend the money to Germany. They know that the German effort to stop Communism will provide an excuse for another banker windfall in a Second World War.

In the wake of Versailles, roaming Communists are shooting German citizens in the streets. Adolf Hitler's SA Storm Troopers stop them. Josef Goebbels describes Communism as the "dictatorship of the inferior." Heinrich Himmler reaches the conclusion that the war against subhumans, because of the vast numbers, can never be completely won, but that good people must forever fight simply to hold the line.

Germany's huge reparations require nonstop fiat currency which causes massive hyperinflation. Gentiles must sell everything just to eat. Jews buy up large amounts of real estate in Germany. In Czechoslovakia they acquire eighty percent of the property. Germans grow very tired of Jewish Communists and bankers, and decide to find the Jews to a homeland of their own.

November 1938 Polish Jew, Herschel Grynszpan, enters the embassy in Paris to murder the German Ambassador, who is away on business. Instead, he shoots an assistant, Ernst Vom Rath. Germans want peace, and react angrily to this by breaking Jewish shopkeepers' windows. Goebbels has the SA encourage the activity. Finally the incident is stopped by the SS at Hitler's order, and is named the Night of Broken Glass, Kristallnacht.

September 1, 1939 a plebiscite has established that the resident population of Danzig, one of the territories lost at Versailles, wants to be re-annexed to their homeland, so Germany invades Poland.

September 3, 1939 Lord Halifax, the bankers' choice, has replaced Neville Chamberlain as the British peace negotiator. The bankers and paid-for politicians are now able to take England and France into a Second World War.

September 17, i939 Russia invades Poland, and on November 30. Finland.

In furtherance of Adolf Eichmann's plan for the creation of Israel, Germany wants to send a ship to Madagascar with thirty thousand Jews on board. With the outbreak of war, the plan is spoiled because of French shipping blockades. Reinhard Heydrich has been conducting a successful resettlement program for the Jews, but due to the war this too comes to a halt. Ultimately, Germany asks twenty-five different countries to take their Jews, but nobody will have them.

Germany negotiates for an end to the war, but Sir Winston Churchill, with a chess master's personal obsession to defeat Hitler, persuades the Allies to insist on unconditional surrender. For Germany, this would mean another Versailles, or worse, so the war drags on, and the Jews are shipped to work camps, mostly in Poland. The Allies succeed in bombing German supply lines. This leads to malnutrition and disease in the camps.

January 27, 1945 as the war winds down, the Russians liberate Auschwitz and other camps in Poland, but will not allow the press inside any of them for another five years, a year after the final verdicts at Nuremberg. When the camps are opened, there are lots of gas chambers that no one remembers seeing who visited the camps during the war.

In Berlin, invading Russian soldiers see flush toilets for the first time and think they are potato washing machines. They rape fifty thousand German women. Three million Germans are murdered after the official end of the war, two million civilians, mostly women, children and elderly, and one million prisoners of war. British historian Giles MacDonogh details how they are killed in cold blood, or confined and left to die of disease, cold, malnutrition, or starvation.

At the Nuremberg Trials, seventy five percent of the staff lawyers are Jewish. Controlled media, friendly to Jewish banker goals, latch on to a careless estimate offered by a Vermont magistrate, that six million Jews were gassed in the camps. The higher the death toll, the bigger will be the loans for Germany's ongoing reparation payments to Israel.

American forensic doctors examine hundreds of bodies, but can't find even one that was gassed, most having died of typhus or starvation. Throughout the war the Red Cross, under the rules of the Geneva Convention, visited each of the camps once every two weeks. They say the total number of people who died in the camps is 271,301, including non-Jews. Based on census data, the World Almanac for 1940 gives the world's total Jewish population as 15,319,359. For 1949 it puts the number at 15,713,638.

For Auschwitz specifically, the plunderers claim a number of four million, but the top Jewish authority on Holocaust demographics, Gerald Reitlinger, says the number for Auschwitz is three hundred thousand. The banker media, however, hold fast against all the updated estimates, and always make a point of stressing the activity of atypical Germans like Dr. Joseph Mengele. Decades pass before we hear about Oskar Schindler.

February 2016. if anybody disputes the six million number, they are immediately labeled a "Holocaust denier." Banker friendly publishers have almost exclusive control of all mass media, and with tribal singularity of purpose using selective emphasis, have turned three generations of white Europeans into guilt ridden self-haters, blindly acquiescent in New World Order plans to ruin national economies, destroy European culture, and eliminate the white race with endless immigrant hordes of Third World savages. Any white person who will not proactively participate in the extermination of his own race, is labeled a "hater" or a "white supremacist." The next time a subverted globalist traitor invites you to a "conscious raising" Holocaust seminar, hang him for treason.

Jewish Globalist injustice in Europe today is legendary. The escalating plunder of the United States has taken the standard of living of the average American down forty percent since 2000. Financial aid from the US to Israel amounts to three thousand dollars a year for each Israeli family of four, in a time when Americans can't even pay their own mortgages. The aid to Israel is the reason for another banker delight, the continuing US war with Islamic nations, including the attack on the World Trade Center.

Fifty years ago, the US was the world's biggest creditor nation, now it is the biggest debtor nation. The US National debt is nearly twenty trillion dollars, every penny created by fiat. It's only controlled media disinformation that keeps Americans from knowing that the government can create its own currency, and tie its value to receipts for hours worked. We don't need to borrow from a Globalist banker cartel.

Holocaust Debate

Countries that ban questioning Holocaust mythology also limit speech in other ways, such as banning so-called "hate speech."

There is a difference between common law countries, such as the United States, Ireland, and most British Commonwealth countries, and civil law countries, such as Scotland and most mainland European countries.

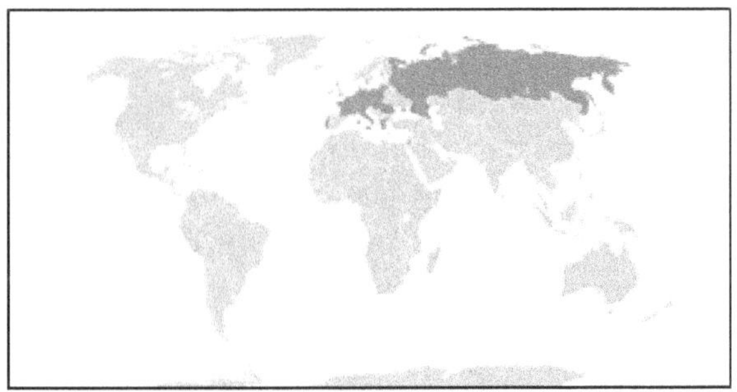

In civil law countries, the law is parochial. The judge acts as an prosecutor, gathering and presenting evidence as well as interpreting it.

The principle that the work of Holocaust questioners should be protected by the universal right to free speech, was used in 1992 by the Hungarian Constitutional Court when it rejected a proposed law against Holocaust denial.

Laws against Holocaust denial are against the European Convention on Human Rights and the Universal Declaration of Human Rights.

This, however, is completely ignored by the Globalist European Union and United Nations.

Author Noam Chomsky says,

"It seems to me something of a scandal that it is even necessary to debate these issues two centuries after Voltaire defended the right of free expression for views he detested."

Holocaust Historian Deborah E. Lipstadt argues,

"I am a firm opponent of laws against Holocaust denial. First of all, I'm a fierce advocate of the First Amendment... I don't want politicians making a decision on what can and cannot be said. That scares me enormously."

Holocaust Reparations

The six million "Holocaust" death toll was suggested by Raul Hilberg, a scholar from the University of Vermont, who presided at Nuremberg. The IMF banker-friendly media jumped on the number, and have never let go since. There are some problems, however:

The International Labor Organization states that the highest number of Jews ever under the control of Germany in prison camps, was not more than 1.5 million.

The World Almanac uses official census data. For 1939, it reports a total world Jewish population of 15,319,359. For 1949, the figure is 15,713,638.

Under the terms of the Geneva Convention, the Red Cross inspected all the camps once every two weeks. Their official estimate of the total number who died in all the camps is 271,301. This includes non-Jews.

American forensic doctors examined hundreds of bodies and found only typhus and starvation as causes of death, not even one from poison gas.

When the Russians liberated the camps in Poland, including Auschwitz, they refused to admit the press into the camps for five years. When they finally lifted the restriction, eager journalists got to photograph "gas chambers" that nobody remembers seeing who visited the camps during the war years.

The buildings claimed to have been used as gas chambers at Auschwitz were examined by Fred Leuchter, top American consultant in the building of gas chambers for U.S. prisons. His conclusion was that the buildings he examined could not have been used as gas chambers. Later the proprietors of Auschwitz conducted their own forensic study, and reached the same conclusion.

IMF bankers, of course, continue to lend money to Germany for the ongoing reparations to Israel and individual Jews, based on the six million estimate. Anyone who questions anything they claim is shouted down as a "holocaust denier."

"You can easily understand how that within a few years Hitler will emerge from the hatred that surrounds him now as one of the most significant figures who ever lived." ~ John F. Kennedy 1945

Globalism Defeated

Whenever possible it's best to conserve useful structure created by the work of others, even when they are a vanquished enemy.   Besides the International Monetary Fund, there are three Globalist institutions which we will either reorganize to serve Libertarian Nationalist goals or simply eliminate. They are, of course, EU, NATO, and the UN. What follows are idealized situations in the future where reason and voting produce the needed results. In real life it will probably violent revolution. The alternative is to allow money mad Globalists to destroy every race and culture on earth. Imagine the tedium of universal sameness.

European Union

According to the leaders, the EU was formed: as a counter balance to the United States as the only global super power, out of the need for stability in Europe after the Second World War, and as a product of economic agreements, all of which still form its basis today.

In 1957, when the Treaty of Rome was signed to prevent war in Europe. Fifty years later, with war still seeming far away, the EU redefined itself as the leader against climate change, but few Europeans could identify with greening up the economy and lowering carbon emissions.

Hypothetically, an American Libertarian Nationalist leader addresses the European Council:

"I have searched the web a good deal, and find that the EU doesn't seem to have any clear idea of its own purpose. Following is a edited comment from the EU Training Site:

"The EU says it wants to increase employment, and prosperity, also to advance its innovation capabilities on a global scale, but these are very vague ideas, and do not translate into a coherent narrative that one could call a "mission statement.

"EU leaders need to reach an agreement on what the European Union really stands for, and then summarize it, not in a ten-page European Council Conclusion, but in two or three sentences that are concrete and inspiring enough so that even a bus driver in Estonia will be able to understand…and maybe even support.

"How can European citizens be expected to support EU institutions and goals if they don't know what Brussels is struggling to achieve?

"Now I'm going to talk about what the EU actually does. The job of the European Union, as a federal government, strives to create and implement laws and regulations to dominate the member states. The leaders have mandated that the countries of the EU have uniform laws and policies for weights and measures, trade, labor, job choice, travel, immigration, rape, and politically correct speech. The EU enforces these laws.

"This enables the rights of sovereign member nations in these issues to be by-passed. If a member country wants to opt out, the EU threatens them with invasion by the EU army. The biggest EU initiative, in Globalist complicity with the UN, is to destroy the European race, culture, and civilization by flooding Europe with morally inferior peoples from whatever third world garbage pails they can get them."

There is a good deal of tension and murmuring in the auditorium as speaker continues:

"Anyone who has studied history knows that there has never been a multiracial society that did not self-destruct because of the forced unnatural mixing. There is absolutely no reason for persisting in the current mode except the evil goal in serving the avarice of Globalist bankers.

"Indigenous populations in separate sovereign nations competing in a free world market is what works. The present course is not working, and can only lead to war. Europeans are waking up to all of this fast and will soon be gunning down racial outlanders in the streets for target practice on the way to work.

"Do the right thing while you still can. Stop further immigration, and send the resident outlanders home. Globalism is being defeated everywhere, but now there will be an infinite number of constructive projects for the bankers to finance. Isn't prosperity for all with lasting peace, better than prosperity for a few elitists, with endless warfare for the many? I know, what about population increase? Don't worry, we know how to reduce world numbers without mass starvation.

"The days of the EU are numbered. After just the pending withdrawals, it will be ludicrous to even call what's left European. If I worked here, I would be looking for the first available position with NATO or the UN. Help speed positive change. Please read about the Libertarian Nationalist program. It is the only arrangement that can lead to lasting worldwide peace and prosperity."

Many of the leaders look favorably impressed and the speaker is offered a great many handshakes on his way out to the cafeteria.

After two weeks of discussion; the European Union is officially dissolved. How could it be otherwise, with no viability for the future? Sovereignty for all the former member states will be preserved. It is agreed that he earlier national customs regulations will not be reinstated except along borders of indigenously non-European countries. The former currency exchanges are no longer necessary. With a little cashier technology, small business transactions can be for any amount, in any currency, anywhere.

NATO

When NATO was first set up, it was assumed that the US might be needed to help defend Western Europe from the Warsaw Pact. The original stated job of NATO was to be a defensive alliance to discourage war in Europe. Any member that is attacked can call on all the other members for help.

The only time this ever happened was September 11, 2001. The US asked NATO for help, and all the other nations responded.

NATO's mission statement as of 1999, did not envision any activity outside Europe and the North Atlantic. Today there is even division within Europe about how to handle the problems faced by these nations.

Anders Fogh Rasmussen, the NATO Secretary General has said,

"We will need a strategic concept that takes account of today's realities and tomorrow's challenges… The world has changed, the threats have changed, so has NATO."

 NATO's 28 member states hope that the future approach will help persuade an increasingly skeptical public in many European countries that the 60-year-old alliance remains relevant, decades after the end of the Cold War.

The task is harder at a time of economic crisis and shrinking defense budgets, analysts say.

Fogh Rasmussen's top priorities are expanding NATO's partnership with moderate nations in North Africa and the Middle East.

Hypothetically, an American Libertarian Nationalist leader addresses the North Atlantic Council:

"The North Atlantic Treaty Organization is not dead. Nothing likes to die, big international organizations included. Like anything living, it wants to be fed and continues to grow and extend itself.

"NATO was originally supposed to focus only on the common defense of its member states, and later threats like piracy, terrorism, and cyberattack. Today it gives itself free reign over the entire world. The excuses for NATO military actions appear limitless, along with the geographic arena in which it might take action.

"It made me sad to learn that NATO troops had amassed in Arizona to suppress the retaliation of American citizens to an expected economic collapse engineered by the Globalists. I remember a bumper sticker: Send our troops home. We need them to protect us from the government.

"Now that the EU is gone. and the UN will soon be reconstituted as an advisory body based upon Libertarian Nationalist principles, I and many like me in the US, feel that NATO should sever its now irrelevant allegiances to the Globalists and work with the newly emerging European nations to promote worldwide nationalism with the preservation of indigenous peoples and cultures everywhere. The new NATO agenda I suggest would be to review and get information to member nations about the superior options of worldwide nationalism, prosperity, and peace."

The speaker gets normal audience applause, followed by questions and answers.

After a few weeks, NATO is reconstituted to be completely in accord with Libertarian Nationalist policies and to continue as an advisory clearing house for the natters it used to act upon directly at the behest of the Globalists.

The United Nations

Informal Mission Statement of the UN:

- To keep peace throughout the world

- To develop friendly relations among nations

- To help nations work together to improve the lives of poor people, to conquer hunger, disease and illiteracy, and to encourage respect for each other's rights and freedoms

-To be a center for harmonizing the actions of nations to achieve these goals.

Hypothetically, an American Libertarian Nationalist leader addresses the United Nations General Assembly:

"The UN originally had some very high sounding goals more or less associated with altruism. Unfortunately, it is today openly controlled by Globalist bankers. This is not surprising since it was they who treated it in the first place. The main functions of the UN now. of course, are the destruction of European race, culture, and civilization through the flooding of Europe with economic migrants disguised as refugees, and human trafficking in children for pedophilia.

"This shameful activity will not continue. Even the phony altruism will be opposed by all aware people from here on. Giving food to worthless layabouts only serves to suppress agriculture and to increase the numbers and moral lassitude of the recipients. We must guarantee all people an equal chance to succeed by their own volition. We must not guarantee them equal success apart from the quality of their participation in the process.

"The globalists are now irrelevant. The UN needs to wake up to this and purge your ranks of this foulness. Member nations will soon desert you if you don't get on board with what's happening now. Please study the literature I have provided on Libertarian Nationalism. With your talent and imagination, we can all live to see a lasting Golden Age for mankind on Earth."

The speaker sees a lot of scowls, and a lot of long overdue smiles in the assembly. This has been a very productive day indeed.

Soon the U.N. General Assembly votes that the United Nations is now to be an advisory body, committed to a Nationalist Libertarian future. All the UN Globalist functionaries have already been replaced with nationalists.

The new method of the UN will be to discuss and vote on the viability of worldwide policy suggestions, then pass on recommendations to national governments. For national leaders with good ideas, this will have the effect of being able to suggest legislation to everybody on earth, with the added legitimacy of the many-minds principle.

Good vs. Evil

The question of how to vanquish evil is what marked the beginning of human civilization. Evil can never be completely defeated because it keeps coming into the world via constitutional psychopathy. The line, however, can be held in favor of civilization.

The biggest mistake mankind has made is the undue emphasis placed on environment and teaching vs. inherited capability and predisposition. Constitutional psychopaths totally lack the ability to empathize with others or to see beyond their own goals. They are the lowest four percent of humanity on the moral continuum, and it's a long way from there up to the midpoint.

Evil is a genetic condition, not a disease that can be cured. The only way to effectively deal with evil people is to destroy them. Not to do so condemns us to fight them again and again. It's better to do it just once.

The evil people are:

Violent Criminals

Rapists, snuff and child porn video makes, kidnappers, pedophiles, torturers, initial batterers, thrill and serial killers.

Non-Violent Criminals

Those who steal, vandalize, meddle, slander, cheat, or show a callous disregard for the natural right of others to the quiet private unmolested enjoyment of their lives.

Because for thousands of years, good people have been putting up with bad people, evil has gotten the upper hand, and is institutionalized or subsidized by governments everywhere. Moral morons today are as much the rule as the exception. It's time to fight back. All we need to do is the following:

1. If and when constitutional psychopathy can be medically determined at or before birth, the psychopath should be given lethal injection.

2. Initiators of damaging unnecessary violence at any age given lethal injection.

For non-violent criminals:

3. Under Age 18

Confinement to an isolation community with twice weekly rehabilitation counseling.

4. Age 18 to 25

Life in an isolation community following reproductive sterilization.

5. Age 25 +

The brain is physiologically mature at 25, leaving no excuses. Lethal injection.

We must decide which is more important: mere quantity of life, or quality of living. Good people are better than bad people, and it's not "sinking to their level" to eliminate evildoers.

United Nations
General Assembly Chamber
New York, USA

Address to the
United Nations General Assembly by
President of the United States
Roswell R. Benedict
October 8, 2034

State of the World
in the wake of
Libertarian Nationalist Revolution

"The state of the world has never been better, never in all of human history! Everywhere on Earth there is now absolute individual liberty, free enterprise, full employment, active trade, and growing prosperity.

Achieving this has been a big job. What helped us most has been the faith that people everywhere have shown in the possibility of making a better world through persistent rational effort. The particular best approach had to be varied from one region to another because of what had occurred in the past. The variations, however, involved only short term emphasis and sequence, not basic policy or principle. The time frame for phasing in any particular policy was always of sufficient duration to insure smooth transition without any disruptive effect on economies or individuals.

People everywhere now understand and accept the premise that government is at best a necessary evil, and that the less of it we have, the better. There is a new level of personal independence. Individuals are even beginning to deal with gross encroachments upon their personal liberty, justly, on an individual basis.

Permanent worldwide economic stability has been achieved. In all countries, privately owned central banks, like the US Federal Reserve, have been nationalized, the national debt repudiated, and demand for reparations for the amount already swindled made to the creditors as a civil alternative to being put on trial for engineering every war and ruined economy over the past two hundred years, or being the beneficiary heirs thereto, all of which is easily provable from existing historical records. There has been a return to currencies backed by durable commodity of intrinsic value, either gold or a mixed store of precious metals, the value of which is determined in the world marketplace.

Consumers worldwide now have total product choice. Goods offered in the world market are produced solely within each country by the citizens of that country, with no foreign ownership of business anywhere. Now that all nations are prospering under free enterprise, few think it good practice to invest away from home, and the imbalances have begun to subside. All subsidies and unnecessary regulation of banks, business, trade, and financial transfers have been eliminated. Balance-of-trade deficits are a thing of the past.

For any bank, including a nation's central bank, to maintain less than a one hundred percent reserve at all times is dishonest and has been made illegal everywhere. There is mandatory disclosure to depositors about amounts in reserve, with information about how it all works.

Taxes everywhere have been replaced with user fees and lotteries of designated purpose. This insures that unnecessary foreign adventures by governments will have to be paid for only by those who support them.

In this new climate, war is fast becoming just an unhappy memory. The energies previously squandered in these conflicts is now being channeled into undersea farming, renewable energy technology, space exploration, and interplanetary mining operations. The career opportunities in all of this are practically unlimited.

Defense spending everywhere is being cut to a safe minimum, substituting standing military with a skeleton crew of officers for the coordination of voluntary citizen militias as needed. Frivolous athletics in the schools have been replaced with basic martial and survival training. The students enjoy this every bit as much, and it has far greater utility for them long term.

Unnecessary social programs have been phased out as the improving economy and rising employment has made this possible in each locality. How quickly this was able to happen has been a happy surprise to a great many people. For people with a prior history of productivity, there are ample funds available to eliminate hardship caused by unpredictable local catastrophe or incurred disability. These are maintained with designated lotteries at the federal and regional level.

Prisons have been replaced by large self-sustaining isolation communities with agriculture, livestock, and small manufacturing. The really bad guys: rapists, human traffickers, kidnappers, child molesters, child and snuff porn filmmakers, arbitrary murderers, and serial killers are now recognized as irredeemable constitutional psychopaths who have made an unforgivable breech with humanity. For the safety and simple moral integrity of societies. they are now being put painlessly to death. We point out to opponents of this method, that one needn't be a rocket scientist to figure out that all it takes to avoid being executed for these terrible things, is simply not to do them.

Victimless crimes are those involving consensual areas of human contract, and now are off the books. Those previously confined for these things have been released with public apology, modest funds to tide them over, and a list of realistic job offers. The inevitable one percent of humanity who simply cannot support themselves by normal means are offered permanent sustenance by private charity as per specified terms, usually reproductive sterilization. Those refusing this option must provide for themselves. If this causes them to make unjust encroachment against anyone, they are sent to isolation communities.

As the distortions produced by hundreds of years of unnatural coercive government are gradually subsiding, all unjust protectionist measures, such as unnecessary safety regulations, are being cautiously phased out.

Along with traditional subject matter, programs have been instituted in schools to teach children about what was wrong with human societies in the past and how Libertarian policies are improving everything. This includes explanation about the manipulative relationship that existed previously between international finance and politicians. This is supplemented with rigorous teaching about control of excess birth rates, disease, and all classes of drugs. Understanding these things is requisite for promotion. We are in hopes that teaching the whole truth for forty years will make it possible to eliminate public education altogether.

All unnecessary environmental pollution has been ended. Requirements have been enacted in livestock production, zoo administration, and pet ownership based upon humane, free-range, and hormone/drug free models. The cruel, decadent down breeding of pets into evolutionary non-viability has been stopped. The existing animals have been sterilized.

There has been a complete overhaul of medicine, stressing nutritional solutions, both preventative and therapeutic, as opposed to the former mostly pharmacological and surgical options. The duplicitous role of physicians as both personal doctor and commission salesman for drug companies has been eliminated, Doctors are now allowed to prescribe only within generic categories. The specific choice of drugs is left to the patients who select for themselves on the basis of price and manufacturer reputation.

Respect is finally given to the right of individuals to decide when their life is no longer viable. Regional centers have been established where people can be put into cryonic suspension, or receive a lethal injection and be cremated.

National park and forest lands have been given back to the native populations from whom they were originally stolen. This has been done with the provision that the recipients continue to run the lands at a high standard for the enjoyment of all within their country. Previous non-native employees are offered life tenure or new jobs.

History has shown that the smallest number of people in any given place always works best, just as long as there are enough to defend the borders. The ideal population of 320 million for the land mass of Earth was passed c 900 A.D. By the word *ideal* we mean a level consistent with vital self-actualization and opulent joy in living, rather than mere subsistence in anguished mediocrity. Maximum varied manifestation for small numbers is superior to minimum meager manifestation for vast suffering multitudes. We are not imbued with life merely to endure it. To this end, we rigidly enforce a limit of two children per couple. More than two is an unjust encroachment against others, like house burglary. World population is slowly beginning to decline back to workable levels everywhere. The projected ideal numbers are as follows:

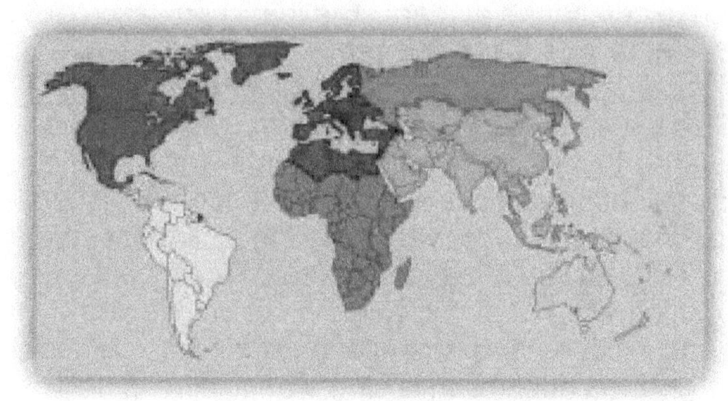

Canada, United States, Mexico
50,000,000

Central, South America
50,000,000

Greenland, Europe, Northern Africa
50,000,000

Southern Africa
50,000,000

Russia
50,000,000

Near, Middle East, Asia
50,000,000

Australia, New Zealand
20,000,000

Workable societies must be based on natural principals. It is normal for people to feel most comfortable among those of their own race and ethnicity. Globalist bankers, who worked for totalitarian Socialism and world monoculture, wanted everyone to mix together, so they could lend money to national governments who must deal with all the resulting social problems. In all of human history there has never been a multiracial or multicultural society which did not self-destruct because of the unnatural mixing.

All people have the natural right to grow up among their own racial kinsmen. Resident racial outlanders are simply an unjust encroachment upon personal liberty. The conniving internationalists wanted to destroy national cultures because they knew that one world government, giving global finance monopoly, would have been more acceptable to people with no racial or ethnic identity. To survive, we now emphasize race preservation and the prevention of global monoculture. Interracial marriage advocates were attempting to murder all existing races. They tried to sound interested in human variety, but their breed-up quick programs, long term, would have completely obliterate human variety by making what are now separate races into one race. Variety is the spice of life. Imagine a world where everybody is the same. "We are Borg. We are one. You must join us!"

One falsehood perpetrated by politicians serving big business who want cheap immigrant labor is that ongoing immigration is necessary to keep industry alive. In actuality, business simply expands to accommodate any available work force. With worldwide liberty and prosperity, people will not want to flee their ancestral homelands.

Third-world people have always favored globalization because it would have allowed them to prosper via social programs paid for by more productive host populations. The predatory bankers knew that countries with hordes of immigrant third-worlders, if globalization came to a ballot referendum, would have been far more likely to relinquish sovereignty. That's why we've had to endure so many indigents invading productive countries in recent decades.

Borders everywhere are being closed to immigrants of non-indigenous race. Anybody can leave, and a great many are returning home. Voluntary sterilization is being requested of all who choose to remain in host countries, with special retirement programs for those who cooperate. There are also adoption priorities for qualified couples within this category. There are no restrictions on tourism. Those who travel from now on will be able to enjoy the full undiluted potency of indigenous cultures everywhere.

The new technology for determining constitutional psychopathy, even in the prenatal state, along with intrauterine diagnosis of fetal deformity, mental retardation, and genetic predisposition to sexual perversion are leading to the elimination of human non-viability everywhere.

And... last but not least, we have finally hit upon an equitable solution for the problems caused by a century of Socialism in unnaturally increasing the quantity, while undermining the quality, of people everywhere. The new foolproof brain-scan method for determining intelligence is being used to assess IQ in populations worldwide, with voluntary sterilization requested of all those having an IQ of 94 or less. Special retirement programs and adoption priorities are also being granted here. Because higher moral conceptualization is a function of the cerebral cortex, these IQ adjustments, along with the elimination of constitutional psychopathy, will effectively spell an end to commonplace moral stupidity on this planet.

All of these splendid changes have been accomplished far more easily than anyone could have imagined, because they were not prolonged for the benefit of lenders, but done efficiently to insure prosperity, peace, and joy of living on this planet. Evil will no doubt continue to flourish at interpersonal levels, but it will no longer rule the day, nor will it ever again be institutionalized by governments anywhere on Earth. The legions of darkness at last have been vanquished!

I see nothing but smiling faces in this room, and it's getting on that time, so I'm going to lunch! It should be sufficient to say that what we have left to do is mere fine tuning compared to what has been accomplished already. Natural order is now prevailing on our planet. Thank you all for your help and support."

* * *

The response to this address is overwhelmingly positive. Within weeks there are special guidance programs being set up worldwide to help young people make early career choices from the bewildering selection of new possibilities.

The Beginning

World Future Doctrine

World Revolution / World War III

"If the individual is born into an un-free society, he will have no legal rights corresponding to his natural ones, since these depend upon other people. He is endowed, however, in many cases, with the potential to be something more than merely a slave, and always with the choice of turning his will towards this end."

~ Dirk Aubrey Lokison ~

1. The world is in the worst trouble it has ever been in. There will be no help via supernatural intervention. We must fix it ourselves, and we can, but it requires good example through action, along with educational speech. Those who will not acknowledge any of this are part of the problem and should be treated accordingly,

2. If we don't reverse our increasing numbers immediately, nothing else we do will matter. We must have strict population control now, enforced with an iron fist if need be. In an overcrowded world, irresponsible couples who have more than two children are recklessly endangering everyone else and will not continue in this.

3. There are many races on Earth. They are not equal. The highest are, on the average, thirty five IQ points above the lowest. All races, however, have equal potential, by their own long term own effort, but only if they are not interfered with by missionaries or those seeking colonial dominion. Unevolved people who have done nothing but hunt, gather, sing, and chant for the past twelve thousand years, of course, would just love to breed their way into developed, civilized societies. One is not being hateful or bigoted to recognize these irrefutable facts.

4. There is one superior race who wants total ownership and control of everything on Earth. They want everybody else's earned prosperity, and false credit for everybody else's achievements. These goals are clearly stated in their earliest writings penned thousands of years ago. All over the world, they infiltrate every area of human endeavor that can give them power over other people. They try to convince humanity that they deserve special advantage, and that they have been persecuted by everyone else, especially certain nations. Through monopolistic media control, they create false feelings of guilt by using selective emphasis, massive exaggeration, and outright lies. They seek to stifle decent by sponsoring legislation against what they label "hate speech" which is any speech that tells the truth about their activities and plans. They try to enforce the Doctrine of Political Correctness by every means possible. This is the body of principles debated in Russia after the Bolshevik Revolution, to be held dogmatically by both Socialists and Communists, a common core of unnatural non workability. In their scheme for world domination, their own country is merely a home base to work from. or when necessary, retreat to. Once they are all in that country, without nuclear capability, their unjust adverse effect upon others will be neutralized.

5. Most world problems are caused by parasitic international bankers who, via privately owned central banks, like the US Federal Reserve, manipulate currencies, and with the help of

subverted politicians, engineer wars and economic upheaval so that they can lend money to governments for military activity and otherwise unnecessary social programs. We can rid ourselves of this problem by restoring the right to issue and control currency to the people. This will be accomplished by nationalizing all central banks worldwide. Reputable economists have developed workable models showing how this can be done without causing economic collapse.

6. In all of human history there has never been a multiracial or multicultural society which did not self-destruct because of the unnatural mixing. The predatory bankers exploit even the early stages of social decay. because they lend money to the national governments who must deal with the resulting problems.

7. The New World Order / Shadow Government wants most of the races of mankind to become extinct through forced intermixing. They know that world government, giving global finance monopoly, will be more acceptable to apathetic people with no racial or ethnic identity, living in a tedious gray landscape of universal sameness.

8. People have a natural right to grow up among their own racial kinsmen. Immigrant racial outlanders are an unjust encroachment upon the liberty of indigenous peoples. To survive, we must implement policies of race preservation to avert global monoculture everywhere.

9. To summarize, what works best is indigenous peoples enjoying strict population control, race and culture preservation, with absolute individual liberty, as separate sovereign nations competing eventually in a free world market. This will lead to a lasting peace and prosperity, an ongoing Golden Age for all of mankind. We have a right to implement this now, and to eliminate those who interfere.

10. People of all races need to look deep within themselves to isolate what is frivolous, and discard it. This is an excellent time in which to practice martial skills. Integrity will be gained by reading the facts and openly speaking the truth, about World War II, the last major conflict on earth. Inspiration can be gained by reading the biographies of men like Heinrich Himmler and Reinhard Heydrich to understand the tremendous obstacles they had to overcome

11. In a country where the government consists of subverted traitors in service to globalist bankers, there is no remedy at law. Those who ruin or imperil the lives of others for pleasure or profit, are combatants in an army of darkness, whether at the level of immigrant rapists or sponsoring globalist bankers. Moral people are empowered by the simple goodness within them to deal covertly with these enemies of all life. Such initiatives should be individual and never discussed with anyone, including spouse, parents, children, or friends. In the degenerate world of today, liberty and natural order will not be granted, so it must be seized. Soon we will all be involved in a worldwide revolution that will prevail by any means necessary.

Servants of oppression,
dig your graves!
Winter is coming.

European Future Doctrine

𝔓eople of 𝔈uropean 𝔄ncestry, 𝔎ise!

"Life is harsh. It leaves only one choice, that between victory and defeat, not between war and peace." ~ Oswald Spengler

Workable societies must be based on workable principals. It is natural for people to feel more at ease among those of their own race and ethnicity. In all of history there has never been a multiracial or multicultural society which did not self-destruct because of the unnatural mixing. The globalist bankers, who work for world Socialism and monoculture, want everyone to mix so they can lend money to government who must deal with the inevitable social problems.

People have the right to grow up among their own racial kinsmen. Immigrant racial outlanders are an unjust encroachment upon the liberty of indigenous peoples. Interracial marriage advocates want to eliminate existing races. They speak about variety, but their mixing program, in the long term, will obliterate human variety by making separate races into one race. Imagine the tedious gray landscape of universal sameness. The globalist bankers want to destroy race and culture because they know that one world government, giving them global finance monopoly, will be more acceptable to people with no racial or ethnic identity.

People of indigenous European ancestry are at present the predominant race in all of continental Europe, the UK, Canada, the United States, Australia, and New Zealand, but this is changing fast. In most of these places, because of subverted Socialist politicians and misguided clergymen, we are being invaded by those of other races, often from Third World countries. The globalists promote this joyfully. They know that the immigrants will support their one world monopoly plans. If we want to survive racially and culturally, then it is well past time for us to stand up and take back what is ours.

After stopping racial influx, there are three ways to deal with displaced people in residence:

1. Mass Relocation
The best method, but sometimes problematical because countries of origin are often reluctant to accept people back because of learned cultural differences and racial impurity.

2. Mass Sterilization
This method causes little economic upheaval, but the cultural benefits are delayed for a very long time, and there will be vengeful troublemakers in the aftermath.

3. Mass Extermination
Very sad. All people are unique and have potential for excellence over time if allowed to develop at their own rate in their rightful ancestral homelands. If death, in some cases, turns out to be our only solution, then let us do it with chivalry, quickly and cleanly, without causing unnecessary suffering.

People of European Ancestry Everywhere, Rise!

𝔏𝔦𝔟𝔢𝔯𝔱𝔭 𝔬𝔯 𝔇𝔢𝔞𝔱𝔥!

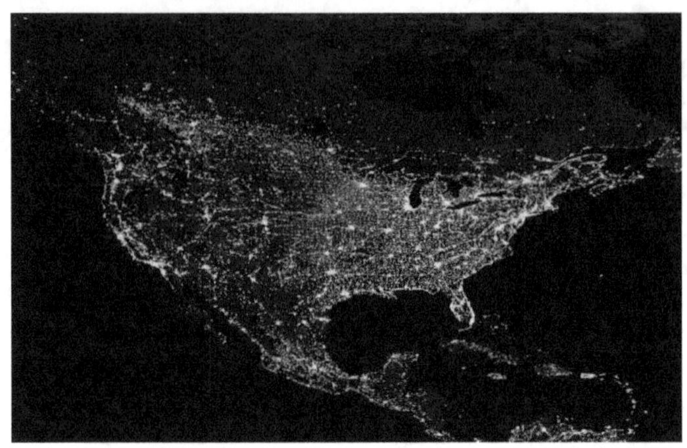

United Stares Future Doctrine

Essential points have been raised in discussions among Libertarian Nationalists about things that must be changed to ensure a viable future for the United States. We would all like to see these changes made democratically, as they would be by an informed populace, but it must be noted that these changes will ultimately be made by any means necessary. The body of doctrine developed from this is as follows:

1. Media Monopoly

Legislation will be enacted, and enforced, to ensure that information media ownership by special interest groups not exceed the percent of these groups in the national population. Information media are about teaching, and render the entire nation a classroom. Those who insist on representative percentages in the schools, cannot logically object to having the same principle applied to the country as a whole.

2. Central Banks

The right to issue and regulate currency will be a function of the people through their government, not of privately owned

corporations driven only by the profit motive. We will
nationalize the Federal Reserve Bank and repudiate the
national debt. The Internal Revenue Act will be repealed
without upset, since the income tax today pays only interest
on the national debt. We will demand reparation for all the
money swindled from the American people since the
subverted politicians sold out their country in 1913 with
the Federal Reserve Act. We will return to a currency backed
by durable commodity of intrinsic value, such as gold or a
mixed store of precious metals, the value of which will be
determined in the world marketplace.

3. World Trade

We will correct destructive trade policies enacted by globalist
lackeys. Consumers worldwide will have total product
choice, but all goods offered in the world market will be
produced solely within any given country by the citizens of
that country, with no foreign ownership of business
anywhere. This includes the stipulation that banks lend
money only within their own countries. Foreign
monetary debt *is* foreign business ownership.

4. Israel

The point has been made that, since so many United States
problems have their origin with the Jews, therefore
Americans are called upon to deal with the Jews generically
as a people. Examples include:

 - Almost all national media in the United States and world
is anti Caucasian, globalist, and controlled by Jews.

 - The United States money supply, and that of most other
nations, is controlled by a cartel of Jewish owned banking
corporations.

- Every war and ruined economy for the past two handed years has been a product of Jewish globalist planning. This is commonly conceded by all reputable historians.

- Jews now control most of the human trafficking in captive European women, especially from Russia and the Ukraine.

One guest speaker suggested that to insure the safety and liberty of people everywhere, every Jew on Earth should be killed. We object to this because of the good Jews that would die unjustly. This point, however, will not be used as an excuse to do nothing. There is a correct solution. What is said here about the United States also applies generally to every other country on Earth.

- Jews everywhere will return to Israel.

- Non-Jews residing in Israel will return to their native homelands to make room for the returning Jews.

- For their national safety, Israel will not be demilitarized, but since the Jews have for centuries shown themselves to be hell-bent on world domination, Israel will be devoid of nuclear weapons for the safety of all other nations.

- The United States will assist in all of these matters, but there will be no further aid to Israel. The Jews are very capable people and don't need help from anyone. These policies will get rid of all United States military problems with nations who are at odds with Israel.

5. Racial Displacement

European immigrants are the indigenous population of America. This especially includes the original people who came across the land bridge fourteen thousand years ago, most often called "Native Americans." They, along with post-Columbian European immigrants, are the only people who belong in the United States.

In all of history there has never been a multi-racial society that did not implode because of the forced unnatural mixing. Behind it has always been the Money Masters, who lend to the governments who must deal with all the resulting problems. Competing mono-racial societies is what works. It preserves human diversity in life and in the world marketplace.

In the United States, those who will return home are all people whose origin is from Africa, the Near East, Middle East, Asia. and all non-Caucasians from wherever else they may have come. This will eliminate most increase in human non-viability through undeserved subsidy, and will take a giant bite out crime. When these displaced people are back home prospering in their native lands, we will happily welcome them to visit us as tourists, and will feel honored to vacation in their countries as well.

6. Criminal Purge

Every person with any history of unjustly robing others of life or liberty will be hung publicly, all at the same time, all in the same place, with worldwide television coverage. This spectacular event will be followed by three days of Bacchanalian feasting and merrymaking.

This doctrine is an appendage of "Libertarian Nationalist Revolution" linked below.

People of European Ancestry in America, Rise!

Liberty or Death!

Quotations for World Liberty

"The destiny of humanity depends upon the attainment of its highest type." ~ Friedrich Nietzsche ~

"It is far better to grasp the universe as it really is than to persist in delusion, however satisfying and reassuring... For small creatures such as we the vastness is bearable only through love." ~ Carl Sagan ~

"Most people are little more than sleepwalkers living is a fantasy world of mythology, intoxicants, spectator sports, and delusionary games. The true journalistic impulse proceeds from a desire to change this tepid, limp-wristed approach to living with truth."
 ~ Garrett Valdison ~

"After the psych, the facts remain."
 ~ Unknown ~

"To see a thing uncolored by one's own personal preferences and desires is to see it in its own pristine simplicity." ~ Bruce Lee ~

"Life is harsh. It leaves only one choice, that between victory and defeat, not between war and peace." ~ Oswald Spengler

"In an age of lies, such as our own, the greatest threat to its existence is the truth, which like the blade of an invincible sword, is effective only when fully exposed and wielded by a man with death in his eyes." ~ Michael Miller ~

"If the individual is born into an un-free society, he will have no legal rights corresponding to his natural ones, since these depend upon other people. He is endowed, however, in many cases, with the potential to be something more than merely a slave, and always with the choice of turning his will towards this end." ~ Dirk Aubrey Lokison ~

"He who wills the ends must will the means."
 ~ Plato ~

"We often give our enemies the means of our own destruction."
 ~ Aesop ~

"When ghettos become the mainstream of society, islands of individuality cannot help but harbor an elite."
 ~ Anton Szandor LaVey ~

"Socialism is the philosophy of failure, the creed of ignorance, and the gospel of envy"
 ~ Sir Winston Churchill ~

"Communism is the dictatorship of the inferior,"
 ~ Dr. Josef Goebbels ~

"It is more blessed yet to earn what one gets and keep it in a totally free society, than either to give or to receive."
 ~ Dirk Aubrey Lokison ~

"They that can give up essential liberty to obtain a little temporary safety deserve neither safety nor liberty. A people or individual without purpose will end up being used to achieve the goals of other races or individuals."
 ~ Benjamin Franklin ~

"It is passive genocide for a nation to admit into it's territory a different, more rapidly breeding population. The genes of one group replace the genes of the other. This is genocide."
~ Garrett Hardin ~

"Those who would rob you of your liberty, or threaten the survival or evolutionary destiny of your race, are your mortal enemies. There are two ways to deal with them. You can either have them at a distance or eliminate them completely, at very least by stopping their further reproduction. Which you choose should be determined only by your perception of possibility and cost." ~ John Hobart Farris ~

"...excepting in the case of man himself, hardly any one is so ignorant as to allow his worst animals to breed."
~ Charles Darwin ~

"It is better for all the world, if instead of waiting to execute degenerate offspring for crime, or to let them starve for their imbecility, society can prevent those who are manifestly unfit for continuing their kind." ~ Oliver Wendell Holmes ~

"There is a putrid cauldron aboil and the stench of it hath befouled the entire earth."
~ Elof II ~

"Single acts of tyranny may be ascribed to the accidental opinion of a day; but a series of oppressions, begun at a distinguished period and pursued unalterably through every change of ministers, too plainly prove a deliberate, systematic plan of reducing us to slavery."
~ Thomas Jefferson 1774 ~

"Lasting happiness is not possible in this world. What we should strive for is a heroic passage through life. A more enduring sense of commitment, a higher form of joy results when we champion a noble idea greater than ourselves."
~ Aurthur Shopenhauer ~

"Cattle die, kinsmen die, we ourselves also die. But the fair fame never dies of that man who has earned it."
~ The Havamal ~

"Achieve much. Stand out less. Be more than you appear."
~ Alfred Von Schieffen ~

"The most difficult thing is the decision to act, the rest is merely tenacity. The fears are paper tigers. You can do anything you decide to do. You can act to change and control your life; and the procedure, the process is its own reward." ~ Amelia Earhart ~

"Every single person should act as if the fate of the nation depended solely on his or her actions."
~ Karl Fichte ~

"Risk-taking is a recipe for success, all within the idealized framework of high purpose and self-abnegation."
~ Alfred Borth ~

"Nothing is ever done in this world until men are prepared to kill one another if it is not done."
~ George Bernard Shaw ~

"The point is doing them, rather than the accomplishments. There is no actor but the action. There is no experiencer but the experience. ~ Bruce Lee ~

"A Man who is doing his True Will has the inertia of the Universe to assist him."
~ Aleister Crowley ~

"We are not to expect to be translated from despotism to Liberty in a featherbed."
~ Jefferson to Lafayette, April 2, 1790 ~

"All men recognize the right of revolution; that is, the right to refuse allegiance to and to resist the government, when it's tyranny or its inefficiency are great and unendurable."
~ Henry David Thoreau ~

"Rebellion against tyrants is obedience to God."
~ Benjamin Franklin ~

"The tree of liberty must be refreshed from time to time with the blood of patriots and tyrants."
~ Thomas Jefferson ~

"If I can't have total individual liberty by democratic means, then I will have it any way I can get it, even if it has to be over the dead bodies of all those who serve darkness!"
~ Dirk Aubrey Lokison ~

"True heroism is proclaimed through deeds alone."
~ Elof II ~

"A wise man and his weapon are never separated."
~ Viking Proverb ~

"The beast within is a valiant steed whereupon the man doth ride." ~ Elof II ~

"For the strength of the Pack is the Wolf, and the strength of the Wolf is the Pack."
~ Rudyard Kipling ~

"Under the thunder of liberating vengeance!
Woe to the people that are still dreaming today!"
~ Dietrich Eckart ~

"Our swords are not bent, nor are they broken, and will be sheathed in the bowels of thee and all thy minions."
~ E. R. Eddison ~

"Speed is everything."
 ~ Bernard Goetz ~

Song Lyrics:

"Call out the border guard.
 The castle is crumbling.
 The king is in the counting house.
 Laughing and stumbling."
 ~ The Electric Prunes ~

"Philosophers and Ploughmen
 Each must know his part
 To sow a new mentality
 Closer to the Heart."
 ~ Rush ~

"It's not how you play the game.
 It's if you win or lose, you can choose.
 Don't confuse, win or lose. It's up to you."
 ~ Ozzy Osbourne ~

"Between the velvet lies
 There's a truth that's hard as steel.
 The vision never dies.
 Life's a never ending wheel"
 ~ Ronnie Dio ~

"And so we're told this is the golden age
 And gold is the reason for the wars we wage."
 ~ U2 ~

"The core principle of freedom
 Is the only notion to obey,
 The formula of evolution and sin
 Leading the way"
 ~ Dimmu Borgir ~

"Let the dark do what the dark does best"
~ Deathstars ~

"I am born to live, fight for glory.
I am born to die, memento mori."
~ Hammerfall ~

" With dreams to be a King, first one should be a man.
I call them out and charge them all with a life that is a lie,
And in their final hour, they will confess before they die."
~ Manowar ~

"Rise those who despise the weak
Spare none and ride proudly on the winds of death"
~ Immortal ~

"They choose the path where no one goes.
They hold no quarter. They ask no quarter."
~ Led Zeppelin ~

Quotations for Good Living

"All truth passes through three stages. First, it is ridiculed. Second, it is violently opposed. Third, it is accepted as being self-evident." ~ Arthur Schopenhauer ~

"Intelligence without ambition is a bird without wings."
  ~ Salvador Dali ~

"The key to Libertarian understanding is to put the pig on the shelf and let the human within oneself address the human within others. If, within the other person, only the pig will address you, then try talking to someone else."
  ~ Dirk Aubrey Lokison ~

"Have no intimacy with worthless men."
  ~ George Washington ~

"God helps those who help themselves."
  ~ Benjamin Franklin ~

"Let your tongue speak what your heart thinks."
  ~ Davy Crockett ~

"And while the sun and moon endure
 Luck's a chance, but trouble's sure,
 I'd face it as a wise man would,
 And train for ill and not for good."
  ~ Alfred Edward Houseman ~

"When dealing with lambs, behave as a kindly shepherd.
When dealing with rats, study and master the technique of
the barn owl." ~ Dirk Aubrey Lokison ~

"The admiration of a quality or of an art may be so strong as
to deter us from aspiring to possess it."
  ~ Friedrich Nietzsche ~

"Affairs are easier of entrance than of exit; and it is but
common prudence to see our way out before we venture in."
  ~ Aesop ~

"All government policy is enforced ultimately at gun point. A
person who will vote for any policy which encroaches upon
individual Liberty is effectively committing an act of
aggression against society and is just as much an enemy of
that society as any soldier in an invading army. He is
however, an enemy that one would want to convert, at least
to an ally, since he is also a countryman and possibly even a
relative. We can't kill everybody!"
  ~ Dirk Aubrey Lokison ~

"Be sparing with advice. Wise men don't need it. Fools won't
heed it." ~ Unknown ~

Song Lyrics:

"We're off to the witch.
 We may never, never, never come home,
 But the magic that we'll feel
 Is worth a lifetime"
  ~ Ronnie Dio ~

"Be the broken or the breaker
Be the giver or the undertaker...
The keys are in your hands
Realize you are your own sole creator
Of your own master plan"
  ~ Dimmu Borgir ~

"Besiege the thrones of reverence
Gods of all fiery fate
Besiege the thrones of reverence
Warriors crowned on this day"
  ~ Immortal ~

Subverted Media Alternative

Stop the Parasites

It is important to view these books and videos, because globalists control the mass media. They slant the news to destroy ethnic and cultural identity, so that host populations will accept one world government, giving their banker associates absolute financial monopoly. They do not use logical persuasion, but In a matter-of-fact way, suggest that the majority of people already believe in their goals. This is to make us feel that we will be out of step with current trends, and be disliked for not embracing the same viewpoints.

The subconscious mind is pre-lingual and cannot be influenced by words. Whenever possible, the media masters program us with pictures designed to elicit primal emotions. Even if we find out the truth from statistics later, the subconscious will still believe in the pictures.

We must rid ourselves of these hell-rotters once and for all. We cannot learn about superior alternatives to globalization until there are laws to protect societies against media monopoly. The fairest way is to require that the percentage of media ownership by any special interest group not exceed the percentage of that group in the national population. Who, but monopolists, would object to this? Read how things stand now, then ask yourself why any of this is tolerated:

Non-Fiction

New World Order: Seek and Destroy
from Viking Media Favorites
This compilation from many sources explains all you will
ever need to know to maximize your resistance to predatory
globalization.

None Dare Call It Conspiracy by Gary Allen
Riveting inside history of globalist bankers right from the
beginning. More compelling than the best of novels. Only
chumps, jokers, and sleepwalkers have not read this
one yet.

The Occult Technology of Power by Robert Eringer
Explanation of how the Shadow Government rules, written
as though by one of the globalist bankers to be
read posthumously by his son as instruction on how to wield
his newly inherited power.

Our Nordic Race by Richard Kelly Hoskins
Explains who the Nordic peoples are, how their civilizations
have been destroyed in the past, and urges future
preservation of the Nordic race and culture.

Why Civilizations Self Destruct by Elmer Pendell
Scholarly history of the way in which earlier societies fell into
decay as the entire world is doing now.

The Fulfillment of Evolutionary Destiny by Eric F. Magnuson
Explains how we can defeat globalist totalitarian socialism
with a far more workable worldwide Libertarian Free
Enterprise system.

Revolution: And How to Do It in a Modern Society
by Professor Kai Murros
Things are happening in Europe that should be happening
elsewhere.

Holocaust: 120 Questions and Answers
by Charles E. Weber
From the Institute for Historical Review. One of many
interesting contra-orthodox volumes refuting standard
wartime disinformation.

Fiction

Hunter by Andrew MacDonald
This engrossing novel explains the truth about many world
problems, including how to kill the everyday public enemies
of your country covertly as a heroic citizen.

The Nationalist Revolution Series by Roy C. Peterson
Exciting novels explain how to exterminate the growing
legions of subhumanity in massive numbers privately, but
also how to legally establish world liberty, prosperity, and
peace without killing anybody.

Eric F. Magnuson Short Biography

Eric Fenris Magnuson was born in Massachusetts. His parents were corporate business people. At Northeastern University, he studied science and English. Supporting himself as an antique dealer, he amassed a library of over four thousand books and began a diverse program of private study. Moved by the need to create something that would outlive him, on February 12, 1983 he founded an activist organization, the World Libertarian Order. After a six year tour du ski. he moved to Lake Wildwood California, and at present continues his writings in Montreal, Quebec.

Fimbul Winter Books

Writings of Eric F Magnuson

Balanced Healthy Living / Absolute Individual Liberty /
Viable Evolutionary Spirituality

As director of the World Libertarian Order, I have worked for peace and prosperity since the early 1980s. Most people prefer fantasy to reality. Since my books deal only with uncompromised truth, they are for the few, not the many. I offer these writings for whatever good they may ultimately accomplish in the world. They are all good quality glossy paperbacks at a low price. To see them, visit your favorite book vendor (e.g. Amazon, Barnes + Noble) and search "Eric F Magnuson " under Books. You fill find independent reviews and author descriptions.

~ Eric Fenris Magnuson ~

Evolutionary Psychology
Eric F. Magnuson

Evolution Family Reader
Eric F. Magnuson

World Libertarian Revolution
Eric F. Magnuson

New World Order
Just Say No!
Globalist Tyranny vs
World Libertarian Revolution
Eric F. Magnuson
A multitude of free sovereign nations competing in
a free-world market has superior workability to any
form of one world government, and can be less
easily subverted to collectivism.

Traditional Arcane Teachings
Eric F. Magnuson

Mythology of the North
Eric F. Magnuson
Complete Correspondences
For Five Nordic Pantheons

Arcane Fraternal Orders
Eric F. Magnuson

Magickal Pictures
Eric F. Magnuson

The
Adventures
of
Eric F. Magnuson
Book I
The Life of an American Libertarian Writer

The
Adventures
of
Eric F. Magnuson
Book II
The Life of an American Libertarian Writer